Paula W
Jo Gustely, RN, BSN, CHPN

MW00830079

DYING WELL
with HOSPICE

A Compassionate Guide to
End of Life Care

Dying Well with Hospice
A compassionate guide to end-of-life care

Paula Wrenn and Jo Gustely, RN, CHPN, BSN

Published by Amans Vitae Press

ISBN 978-0692945087

Praise for Dying Well with Hospice

"This is truly an exceptional book, chock-full of depth and insights in the practical as well as the emotional/spiritual realities one will encounter as a patient and loved one facing a life-threatening and ultimately terminal illness together. Dying Well with Hospice provides a wealth of wisdom and advice to those living these pathways, skillfully blending the experience of the lay family member/caregiver and the professional. I am very impressed and would recommend this book to all of our patients and families as well as to young professionals considering or starting out a career in medicine. In fact, Dying Well with Hospice would be a valuable and touching learning experience for well-established professionals. The authors' insights and heart are so evident in this work".

Gary Johanson, MD
Palliative Care Services
Medical Director, Memorial Hospice and Home Health

"In Dying Well with Hospice, Wrenn and Gustely provide an excellent and unique resource for patients, families, and friends of the terminally ill. In addition to Wrenn's insightful perspective on the emotional and spiritual dimensions at the end of life, there is also a wealth of practical pointers on dealing with the innumerable daily challenges for both patients and caregivers. Gustely exhibits obvious compassion and in-depth knowledge of the process of dying as well as effectively alleviating suffering. Her viewpoint as a hospice nurse provides a clear and persuasive argument for those dealing with terminal illness to avail themselves of hospice care at an early stage in order to achieve peace and comfort in this final transition. As a physician, I *highly recommend this extremely informative book to those dealing with severe or incurable illness, as hospice care is very effective and most often sought too late in the course of illness".*

Niranjana Parthasarathi, MD
Retired Associate Professor of Clinical Internal Medicine
University of Cincinnati College of Medicine

"As a long-term caregiver to my wife who was on hospice for two years, I wish I could have read this book before my caregiver role began. The self-care recommendations and important tips for spousal caregivers are invaluable. Dying Well with Hospice *has essential information about the dying and grieving processes. It will be a useful guide for any friend and family member who is supporting or will support a terminally ill loved one."*

Joachim Kothe
Spouse and caregiver

*"*Dying Well with Hospice *is a most valuable guidebook for those facing death and those caring for them, as it reinforces the vital message that none of us are alone in our lives or at the end of our lives. The diary format is delivered to the reader with a strong aura of personal strength exhibited by Jim and Paula, and supported by the kind and caring professional assistance of Jo, the hospice nurse. Advice given and lessons learned as they progressed down the road at the end of life are carefully and meticulously shared in this extraordinary volume. I would recommend it to friends and family members."*

Janne E. O'Neil
Estate Planning Attorney

"What is important to experience as we die is the conversation we avoid most in our society—the exchange of feelings, thoughts and wishes with those we love and who will support us during this emotional time. Dying Well with Hospice *gently encourages us to find peace by thinking forward and planning in advance for our comfort and care in the final months and days. As a former therapist who worked with the dying and grieving, an avid reader and an advocate for my local library system, this book is an invaluable resource for all libraries, home and public".*

Reece Stauffer Foxen, MA
Life Coach

"Dying Well with Hospice *is filled with meaningful personal stories and compassion around end of life. It is a must-read for everyone who has relatives or loved ones who are seriously ill, aging, or dying."*

Ziad Hanna, DO
General Surgery

"The authors of Dying Well with Hospice *fully illustrate why it is important for Americans to get over our squeamishness around the subject of death so we can live our lives as fully as possible to the end. This book offers a touching story of one couple's end-of-life journey, together with practical contributions from the hospice nurse who saw them through it. It is valuable and healing.* Dying Well with Hospice *is an important read for any adult who has yet to make end-of-life plans."*

Deborah Howell
CEO, Alexander Valley Healthcare

Acknowledgments

Working for twelve years alongside the caring and consummate care providers of North County Hospice, a branch of Memorial Hospice in Sonoma County, California, has expanded my knowledge and skill as a nurse. Additionally, my hospice clients and families have helped me become a better person and a better support to other patients.

I am eternally grateful to my parents, who provided me with a priceless education, and especially to my mother for the valuable life lessons that set me on paths of enrichment in my career and personally. Finally, I want to posthumously acknowledge Jim Ronlund, Paula's husband, for making this project possible. Not only did he ask her to write about his journey, he encouraged us to develop our friendship, which led to this collaboration. – Jo Gustely

My unending appreciation goes to all the loved ones who have gone before and revealed to me many lessons about end-of-life choices. I am grateful to author Gary Zukov, whose work helped me validate my ideas of spirituality so that I could be fully present as my husband's amazing final journey unfolded. My friend, Dini Alves, added much to my knowledge about caregiving long before I ever needed to put it into practice.

Jim's hospice team from North County Hospice was as much a lifeline for me as it was an aid for Jim to successfully complete his journey. We were fortunate to have the most compassionate and competent health care professionals throughout Jim's journey. There are no words to thank Ziad Hanna, DO, for his sage advice that guided us through two years of grief and joy. I also want to thank our friends and family who stood by us during the journey and supported us—you mean so much to me.

My co-author's contributions and support on this effort made it possible for me to make good on my promise to Jim. Jo and I are grateful to friends and associates who believed in our project and gave us feedback. We also are so happy that we found Howard VanEs from Let's Write Books, Inc., whose expertise guided us in making our book a reality. – Paula Wrenn

Foreword

The hospice movement has been nearly 50 years in the making in the United States, yet many Americans believe that life and death are the realm of the health care system and something over which they have absolutely no control. When there is no room in the belief system of the patient or family for hospice, particularly when cancer is the diagnosis, many feel that continuing to "fight" is the only (acceptable) course of action. In fact, over-extended or unnecessary treatment does not benefit the patient. It adds to distress, debilitation and exhaustion, as well as using up precious time needed to prepare emotionally for the inevitable death. Unnecessary treatment is a drain on the average American's personal finances as well as the health care system.

The decision to treat and when to stop treatment should be an ongoing conversation between a patient and the health care team. For their own reasons, some will want to fight for a little more time, despite odds that doing so will endanger their quality of life for the limited time left. Those of us who have seen patients' lives transformed by hospice understand how important it is to continue getting the word out about the physical comfort, emotional support, and relief hospice brings not just to patients, but to their families. When quality of life becomes the focus, the patient is truly benefitted.

But what about the patient who has not put their wishes in writing, and who is not of capacity to give consent to stopping treatment? There are many patients in skilled nursing facilities around the country whose families do not know how to advocate for them. A patient who is fully incapacitated by disease, injury or dementia before making known his or her wishes for end-of-life care may be trapped along with their families in an extended and costly downward spiral that most who observe it would conclude is cruel. Who among us wants to be kept alive when we cannot enjoy life? This is one of many important discussions in *Dying Well with Hospice*.

I so deeply identified with *Dying Well with Hospice*, sometimes coming from the place of being a former hospice caregiver, and sometimes recalling my personal experiences caring for my own mother and mother-in-law, as well as elderly friends. Jo Gustely and Paula Wrenn both share deeply and fully with their readers of their personal and intimate experiences, observations and insights encountered when privileged to engage with hospice patients. Having read many books on dying and hospice care, this is the first I have encountered that tracks the entire journey of one patient/couple from both the personal and professional perspectives. *Dying Well with Hospice* treats a difficult subject with dignity, compassion and even humor. Readers will see that when couples and individuals are open to support during the meaningful transformation from life to death, joy is part of the journey and can help prepare the hospice patient to move on. I believe *Dying Well with Hospice* also illustrates that joy can be found in the challenging work of caregiving, and following the loss of a loved one.

Dini Alves
Former Publisher, *Caregiver Magazine*

Table of Contents

Introduction 7
Chapter One – Dying 11
   The Question 11
   The Gift of Truth 13
   Unexpected Gifts from the Dying 15
   Lessons about Death and Grief 19
   Damages of Denial 20
   My First Hands-On Hospice Experience 22
   A Deathbed Resolution 24
   Mom's Delivery from Dementia 28
   Discussing Mortality is Not Morbid 30
   Chapter Summary 31
   Resources 32
Chapter Two – Planning Ahead 33
   Growing Old is a Privilege Denied to Many 33
   Planning to Die at Home 37
   Planning is a Loving Thing to Do 39
   Put Your Plan in Writing 42
   Written Directives Can Reduce Suffering 44
   The Added Consideration of Dementia 46
   Plan for Your Own Infirmity 48
   Financing Late-Life Care 49

When Family is Far Away 55

Consideration for Fears of Dying 60

Aid in Dying. 61

Voluntary Stopping Eating and Drinking (VSED) 62

Funeral Planning 64

Chapter Summary 67

Resources 69

Funeral information 70

Chapter Three – The Dragon Year **71**

Something is Wrong 71

Unraveling the Mystery 77

Not-So-Merry Christmas 79

Other-Worldly Guidance 82

Being my Best for Jim 86

Jim Plans for His Family 88

Treatment 91

A Metaphor for Strength and Wisdom. 93

Processing Treatment Options 95

A Wild Getaway 97

The Medical Roller-Coaster Ride 101

Finding our New Normal 104

Burying Jim's Parents 106

Goodbyes and Gifts. 107

Reasons to Celebrate the Diagnostic Anniversary 109

The Option of Palliative Care 111

Chapter Summary 112

Resources 114

Chapter Four – Living **115**

    Friends 115

    Change on the Way .117

    Good Days, Bad Days 119

    Making the Best Choices to Support Daily Comfort 124

    The Big Shift 124

    Decline and Devotion 128

    Many Goodbyes 129

    Celebrating 132

    The Biggest Adventure 136

    Chapter Summary .145

    Resources 147

Chapter Five – Caregiving, Diagnosis to Death **149**

    Caregiver Self-Care .151

    Hospice Patient Needs 153

        Client Personal Care 153

        Meal management 154

        Motility 154

        Home management 154

    Your First Day as a Caregiver 154

    Patient Receptivity .156

    Appropriate Caregiving Help 157

    Care and Help Alternatives 160

    Be Flexible 161

    Know Your Limits 162

    Caregiving from a Hospice Perspective 164

    Chapter Summary .169

    Resources 170

Chapter Six – Death delivered comfort, peace and healing . . **173**

The Distraction of Fear 173

Active Dying Approaches 175

The Sands of Time Run Low 181

Signs Death is Near 184

Our Final Goodbye 186

Vigil or Absence? 187

My First Day without Jim 188

My First Week Alone 189

First Months: A Time to Grieve 190

Comforting the Bereaved 192

My First Solo Challenges 194

Moving on with Help from Jim 197

Chapter Summary 204

Resources 206

Dedication **209**

Lyrics to *Gathering* **composed by Karen Joy Brown** **210**

About the Authors **212**

Introduction

We don't have a choice about death; it is going to happen.

Dying well, that is to say, comfortably and peacefully, may be the most important and most misunderstood topic in the realm of personal choice. So why are we afraid to speak of it, much less actively plan for it? Many people in the United States are unwilling to speak of death, though most everyone who dares to do so will say they want a peaceful death. Surely, you have heard more than one person say, "I want to die in my sleep." Unfortunately, the conversation seldom goes deeper.

What many adults fail to realize is that those of us who will experience a natural death following a period of decline or terminal diagnosis do have a choice about whether we go peacefully or whether we suffer. *Dying Well with Hospice* is written for adults who want to give thought to dying peacefully or who want to know how to support others they love in doing so. When the dying individual is a family elder, knowing those left behind can handle bereavement is also a factor in their acceptance and peaceful crossing over. When a dying patient is well cared for using the variety of resources and techniques proven to facilitate a peaceful transition, family members involved in that phase of the patient's life often have an easier time with grief because they are with their loved one as the natural process unfolds until they can see and accept that the time has arrived for their loved one to leave.

Dying Well with Hospice is about practical ways to approach natural death following a terminal diagnosis. It is geared toward adults middle-aged and older. It does not promote aid in dying (legally accelerated death), though reference is made to that topic in comparison with natural death. This is not a book about sudden death or decisions to be made for young people, though readers may glean some ideas that are applicable to those situations. It is not written with a specific religious doctrine in mind but promotes supporting the religious or spiritual beliefs of the dying. It further serves to reveal valuable life lessons the authors have gained while caring for terminal patients and to express the grace and comfort bestowed on terminal patients and their loved ones through dignified end-of-life care.

Throughout Jo's experiences as a hospice nurse seeing a panoply of choices people have made about dying, she was able to gather pearls of wisdom to share from watching people's final weeks about how families make choices during that time. "I feel as though there remain gaps in people's knowledge base that result in a lot of preventable suffering. I have a sense of urgency to explain why we have to be able to talk about this more easily and more often. We have to talk about our own death so others are aware of our needs and aren't left guessing what we want at the end of our lives."

Previous experiences with death and hospice were helpful to Paula when it came time for her to care for her terminally-ill husband. As a writer, she sensed there was much to be shared about this important time of life, but it was when her husband asked her to write about their shared journey that she realized his full appreciation for hospice and the way they were able to manage his end time. "Jim also facilitated me staying in touch with Jo after his death, you'll read about that, so I was eventually able to see that my memoir of that time would be strengthened with Jo's expert contribution and insights, thereby giving the reader a more complete understanding. I was motivated to write this book to fulfill my husband's desire to help others by telling his story."

Our over-arching goal in writing this book is to dispel the myth that terminal patients who choose to end treatment have "given up." Instead, it is about how the end of life can be embraced fully when the distractions of treatment are removed at the choice of the patient, thereby allowing terminal individuals to decide what they want to do with their remaining time. We hope readers will finish the book with the understanding that preparing to die and supporting someone else through end of life is about personal growth and enlightenment. Giving thought to how you want to die and making your wishes known is both productive and freeing.

* * *

To assist readers in following who is "speaking" at various times throughout the book, readers should note that Paula Wrenn's story is told in regular font, and Jo Gustely's personal and professional contributions are denoted using italics.

Chapter One

DYING

"A man has only one death. That death may
be as weighty as Mount Tai, or it may be as light
as a goose feather. It all depends upon the way he uses it."
- Sima Qian, astrologer and historian, Han Dynasty, c. 98 BC

THE QUESTION

His body shrunken and face gaunt, his hazel eyes remained steady and clear as he looked into mine and calmly asked, "What will it be like when I finally die?"

Today's question was the crux of my purpose in our relationship. On this day, his increasing frailty made it appear as if his masculine leather easy chair had grown larger around him. Of late, he had taken to wearing pajamas all day and seemed easily chilled. Having recently given up venturing to the porch to sit, he was quickly approaching the time he would not leave his bed. Over the previous four months we'd had many honest and difficult conversations as Jim continued his journey toward the final transition.

His wife Paula sat nearby and I began my response as I had many times before for other hospice clients, first explaining that the vast majority of hospice patients experience pretty much the same process. "The body knows exactly how to wind down. It is programmed to secrete hormones that aid in the process," I began.

Human death is similar to the way in which other mammals naturally leave this life. I asked Jim if he recalled a pet dying of old age, and how the pet may have shown less interest in activity and eating until it finally withdrew to a corner or crawled under a bush before gently going to sleep. Akin to that, I explained, he too would slowly withdraw from his interests and lose his desire to eat.

Jim listened intently as I continued to describe that he would simultaneously feel more tired than usual and that he would take more frequent, longer naps. Eventually, he would ingest only small bites and sips of nourishment. Once the desire to eat and drink are eliminated by the body's hormones, napping would catch up to nighttime rest until he would sleep around the clock.

Most of his muscles and reflexes, including swallowing, would become relaxed. His wife and care-givers would focus on his comfort, keeping him clean, repositioning him and administering comfort medications, if needed. These would reduce any symptoms such as pain or labored breathing. His hearing and his subconscious would remain active, so he would hear visitors saying their goodbyes or loved ones speaking to him. He could have vivid dreams and see loved ones that had died before him. Sometimes breathing is louder than normal. A small number of patients have moist, heavier breathing near the end. Brief, wakeful moments are not unusual, but following his final intake of liquid, his heart would stop in his sleep within two weeks.

Throughout this process, hospice would guide his family, teaching them in advance of each step how to protect his dignity and assure his comfort. Hospice staff and I would be increasingly present to support everyone, as well as to continue our support for the family after his transition. To his family, he would most likely appear calm and have a peaceful expression on his face during the final hours. Some hospice patients appear to glow and smile slightly as though they have experienced something wondrous or awe-inspiring. I watched as Jim quietly took in this information.

It is received as good news when I tell patients that we tend to fade away gently and quietly in our sleep. As with many other patients and families I have guided through this process, Jim's relief was visible once he had the information he needed. Paula also appeared relieved as Jim took everything in and thanked me for being straightforward. If we imagine our final transition in advance and clearly make known our wish for support during the process, we are far more likely to achieve it. Jim's relief at this description of his imminent death isn't surprising when you consider that passing quietly in one's sleep is what nearly everyone describes they would like. That is what hospice facilitates.

THE GIFT OF TRUTH

What is it like to die? The question is often internalized but seldom verbalized. How ironic that an experience so important and universally pondered is seen as taboo where modern medicine is practiced, especially in the United States, where it is virtually banned from everyday discourse.

My friend and co-author, Jo Gustely, along with her colleagues in hospice organizations around the country, is in a unique position to answer this question in the course of providing aid and comfort services to hospice clients and families. That is not to say that all hospice patients ask about or even care to acknowledge impending death. However, given adequate time to develop trust with their hospice providers and to accept the inevitability of death, many hospice clients genuinely want to know about their process. Those who have thought about their death process may be more comfortable and even curious as to what is ahead for them.

In our conversations regarding why the general population is so averse to addressing the topic of death, Jo has pointed out to me that many people are never exposed to a natural death because fewer people die at home than even just fifty years ago. She also shared that she believes fear and misunderstanding of dying is exacerbated by visuals of violent deaths depicted every day in cartoons, movies, and on television.

Jo was my husband's hospice nurse. His trust in her was a wonderful comfort to him and to me. Of course, hearing Jo explain the specifics of dying was not the first time since Jim had become sick that we had to listen to difficult information. There had been many days and many layers of bad news following the first doctor's appointment at which his primary care physician directed us for more tests. But by this time, about twenty-two months later, we had learned that there is always some sort of comfort in having the truth. Sad as it was to receive disappointing news about his condition, we always eventually found consolation in our relationship. Each time there was bad news, it was followed by a period of grieving as we absorbed the new information regarding each challenge to Jim's longevity. We would then learn something important to share with or support one another.

But this time, this question, was different for me. This was the ultimate question about the final moments of his life. I can't say how Jim felt in the moment, but I can tell you I was very concerned for his reaction to the response. When Jim asked Jo what it's like to die, she and I exchanged brief glances as if to say, "This is it." I then leaned in to learn her response, wondering what she could possibly say to his direct and double-edged inquiry; he needed to know what he wasn't sure he wanted to know. All the time ready to comfort my husband should it be too much for him to bear, I soon realized Jo's calm, gentle voice delivering the complete answer was all he required in that moment. As I had witnessed numerous times before, having difficult questions answered removed his distraction so Jim could once again refocus on living his remaining days.

UNEXPECTED GIFTS FROM THE DYING

Sometimes good, even great, things come from our worst personal tragedies. Though my mother's time in hospice was limited, I was able to be there and witness her transition and the rare way in which she achieved resolution of emotional pain before her death. Her story is unusual because the compressed timeline required her to find resolution in just thirty days between diagnosis and death. Fortunately, many terminal patients have the opportunity for more time in hospice.

If the patient can put fear aside and come to hospice before beginning to withdraw from friends and activities, they can reap the full physical and psycho-spiritual benefits of hospice. The first big benefit to a hospice patient is the attention to and reduction of physical pain and suffering. Early entry into hospice also affords greater educational and interventional assistance for family members and caregivers learning how to be the best support. Finally, if there is enough time, the patient can experience the healing of old emotional wounds and the release of old beliefs to find true healing and happiness as they are released from this life. Hospice nurses advocate for careful, conscious preparations for entering hospice at an appropriate time. An appropriate time is usually months before the expected end of life or when the patient's bad days begin to outnumber good days (determined in consultation with the patient's physician). Later in this book we discuss specific ways to know the right time for your family to seek hospice assistance.

Every human experiences emotional pain. Many of us seek resolution of past painful experiences throughout life. However, it isn't until near death when it seems a miracle sometimes happens that enables resolution of particularly difficult emotional pain. As a hospice nurse, I have watched clients who are seemingly hours from death cling to life longer than one would think possible. Even if they are unconscious, the last-minute farewell visit of a child may bring that resolution so death can come peacefully in a few minutes or hours. I have been extremely privileged to witness transitions from fearful to a state of peace as clients replace false beliefs and hurts with forgiveness and gratitude. What I want to share with you is my own personal experience of how differently patients work toward resolution and how one event directed me toward a hospice career. My own mother's case was unusual and illuminating.

By the time she reached her early seventies my mother had lived with Parkinson's disease for nearly a decade; her mind and balance slowly failing. At age seventy-three her belly was enlarging while her limbs and face seemed unnaturally thin and gaunt. Despite a lifetime of being trim and eating small meals, she suddenly developed a ravenous, near-manic appetite. She could not tell us why she was wasting away. One October day, she became suddenly so short of breath that she was taken to the emergency room. The emergency room doctor told my parents while reading the white images on the x-ray that my mother was full of masses throughout her chest and belly. Days later, when the oncologist told her there was no cancer treatment that would prolong her life, she immediately cried. As a registered nurse, she knew the breadth and locations of her tumors meant she was dying, so she wasted no time preparing for her death. The next day she started notifying family members of her terminal illness.

The very moment I heard my mother was being placed on hospice, I took a leave from my nursing job and moved into her home to care for her. Though I still had an empty feeling for her after forty-five years of a troubled relationship, something told me that caring for her was the right thing to do. Throughout my life I had often wondered how I would deal with my mother when she died and whether I would feel deep sadness and sympathy. Now that she was dying, I indeed felt genuine sadness. On the second day of caring for her, my mother required assistance with what turned out to be her final shower. After undressing her emaciated, naked form, a radical shift took place in my heart. A wave of compassion washed over me as I contentedly administered to my now-dependent mother. This vulnerable human was no longer the abusive mother of my childhood but someone who deserved the most dignified care before she died.

Two days before her death and already in a coma, my mother began to sob. Her eyes would not open and she did not speak. As instructed by the hospice RN, I used prescribed doses of comfort medicines to try to relieve the sobbing. Was she grieving her own painful childhood of physical and emotional abuse that she had often told me about when I was small?

As a child, having been shown the scars of abuse on her body, I now sensed she absolutely had to sob to release a lifetime of buried, festering sorrow. I believe her consciousness urgently needed release from emotional pain due to the short time span between diagnosis and active dying. Perhaps she also needed to release her guilt at the pain she caused her own children when she continued the cycle of abuse. She may also have grieved her own accelerated death. My tenderness toward her grew as I observed her continuous weeping.

I felt certain this was necessary so she could die in peace. Her despairing sobs spontaneously ceased after about six hours. The following day, just thirty days after her cancer diagnosis and one week after I arrived, she quietly died with her family encircling her.

I cannot explain more about my mother's transition than I have. I could never have predicted how profoundly caring for my dying mother would change me. All I can tell you is I was relieved of the burden of our troubled relationship to a large degree, having witnessed her sorrow. Perhaps thrusting myself fully into caring for her as she swiftly deteriorated and embracing her ever-increasing suffering broke my heart open. When I came away from that tumultuous crisis, I found I was not so easily upset by the dysfunction of family dynamics. I was far more patient in dealing with my autistic brother's communication challenges. Slowly, over time, I gained the distinct impression I could actually feel my heart. Though my professional self was kind and caring, I saw myself becoming inwardly more tolerant and more humane.

It has been a benefit to me to see how important it is to have resolution before death. I have adopted a personal mission to advise others to consider working on unfinished business and forgiveness before death is imminent. Observing my mother's healing at her time of death redirected my hospital-based nursing career; I became a hospice nurse hoping for similar healing for my clients.

Over the next ten years I read about and researched dying and the growing hospice movement. Studs Terkel's book Working *motivated me to look for my highest, most meaningful career potential. In the change to hospice work I found the intimate and delicate nature of the work provided the meaning I longed for in my career. Acknowledging the rarity of spiritually fulfilling work, I give thanks to all, especially my mother, for guiding me towards it.*

As a hospice nurse, I have witnessed hundreds of deaths, but I have never heard of nor seen again this unconscious, prolonged sobbing and grieving in a hospice patient prior to death. What I have infrequently observed is patients becoming animated with restlessness of varying degrees, or vocalizations, as they work through past pain and hurts. Observing this can distress family members. In anticipation of this infrequent occurrence, hospice provides the family with a "comfort kit" of medicines and remedies. The family can call hospice at any time for guidance in using the kit to help the hospice patient rest comfortably.

Finally, my mother had little time from diagnosis to death, so her immediate acceptance of impending death made it possible for her to come to resolution in such a short time. However, patients who have three to six months of hospice support are more likely to have full benefit and resolution from their hospice experience for themselves and their families.

LESSONS ABOUT DEATH AND GRIEF

At his open-casket funeral, Grandma wanted me to pat Granddaddy's hand. I loved my grandfather but was aghast at my first sight of a dead person at age twelve. I began to wail after she placed my hand on his unnatural, waxy skin. This embarrassed my mother and earned me a tense and threatening lecture in the mortuary restroom. Aside from fear of being judged unworthy of a heavenly afterlife, I can't recall more specifics of my fear of death, but it stayed with me well into young adulthood.

My next death experience was Mom's father. He had been in a care home in North Carolina for a couple years and I did not have the opportunity to see him. I was in my early twenties and absorbed with getting my young adult life on a good track both personally and professionally. At that time, I may have felt it was someone else's job to look after dying members of the family. As we traveled to his funeral, my mother cried only briefly, lamenting her "Papa" would not see my brother graduate from college. Her stoic expression then returned and I never saw her cry again. I was sad and still afraid of dying but not as dramatic about this granddaddy's death because the adults all seemed to feel it "was for the best." I was learning to mask my fear of death as the adults around me were doing.

DAMAGES OF DENIAL

By age seventy-four my father began to have serious health issues that eventually led to a terminal diagnosis of non-Hodgkins lymphoma. An aunt's illness and death before my father's diagnosis had already revealed my mother had deep-seated fears surrounding death. Perhaps she inadvertently influenced my early fears.

Because my mother chose to "believe in miracles" and not acknowledge Dad's diagnosis as terminal, information my siblings and I received was selective and not necessarily accurate, but I felt Dad might not be alive at the same time next year. We arranged a full-family Thanksgiving as he always wanted us all to come together at their house. Being scattered around the country, this effort had seemed too difficult until we siblings were faced with this urgent circumstance. We hoped it would be a memorable Thanksgiving on many levels and a boost to Dad's spirits. It was quickly obvious to us that something our mother once would have relished was overwhelming and upsetting to her on top of her caregiving duties.

Mom's world had been turned upside-down by developments with her spouse's health and the rigors of caregiving. Early signs of her dementia began to show up as inflexibility and inappropriate anger. She swept and cleaned constantly, never sitting down to socialize or be with Dad. She loudly chastised a grandchild for asking for a second cookie, putting her arms possessively around a box that possibly contained more than four dozen cookies. "We won't have enough to last the weekend!" she exclaimed.

Worst of all, she remained steadfastly in denial about my father's terminal diagnosis. Fortunately, cousins who lived near my parents kept us informed after we returned home. Mom was so resistant to the truth that she wanted to fire a doctor who tried to help her accept the reality of our father's status. Essentially, our father continued treatment at Mom's insistence that they might receive a miracle, despite the treatments worsening his condition, eroding his quality of life in heartbreaking ways. When I suggested hospice to my mother, she was alarmed. "Oh no, that's for dying people!" was the unfortunate response. No amount of reasoning or logic would cause her to abandon her belief that there was a miracle with Dad's name on it.

The lesson I was learning at this time was that some adults really do fear death, but the evidence is often behind the scenes. It can be mixed up in their belief system or covered over with seemingly good intentions that can be harmful.

It was their choice, but it bothered me that my mother insisted Dad continue to take treatment for cancer until the treatment was doing more damage than good. Ultimately, my father was so sick and weakened he landed in the hospital, and I believe my mother thought he would soon be well enough to come home again. When it became apparent to my siblings that Dad was actively dying, my older brother took Mom home and my younger brother remained with Dad so he would not be alone in the impersonal hospital environment. He died that night. Sadly, once Dad was gone, we began to understand that my mother's early dementia contributed to her fears and directed her choices. With Dad gone, Mom's world changed dramatically and she began to deteriorate at an accelerated rate.

Both Jo and I have seen how denial works against one's ability to process the steps toward a peaceful transition. Sometimes the patient is in denial, sometimes the spouse. There can be an entire family system of denial where death and illness are never mentioned and everyone seems to be surprised when death occurs. We find this particularly sad because important things are left unsaid. A family who misses out on seeing a peaceful death process for a loved one may find it more difficult to be at peace with the loss and with realistically accepting their own impending death at a later time.

MY FIRST HANDS-ON HOSPICE EXPERIENCE

At the beginning of 2005, I helped an aunt and uncle relocate from Oregon to live in my small community. Uncle Ben had suffered a stroke, so it was a nice arrangement for them. The first two years were light duty for me and a blessing for them in terms of greater independence and accessibility to things they needed.

My caregiving and companionship efforts were focused on my aunt and uncle, but I also visited a friend who was on hospice care, finally ready to stop battling recurring cancer. Jan and I had some good visits and I admired how she kept herself engaged with her grandchildren. She wanted visits to help her "feel normal," so we laughed and cried and I watched her make use of the services hospice offered her. She seemed to have a healthy and relaxed outlook. Jim and I would discuss my visits with her, agreeing that her acknowledgement of impending death seemed to afford her the opportunity to live as fully as possible. She had obtained some pills in case she could no longer bear living. I don't know whether she took them, but it gave her comfort to have them. It was less than two weeks from the time she ended visits that Jan passed away.

In 2007, Uncle Ben's health took a sudden sharp turn with a trip to the emergency room and a hospitalization that led to hospice. Uncle Ben's last two weeks of life were spent at home under hospice care. Barbara was caught off-guard by his sudden decline. Not only was she distraught, she was not someone inclined to caregiving. Fortunately, some of the same hospice professionals that tended to my friend Jan were also on Uncle Ben's hospice team, so I knew the compassionate support my uncle and aunt would receive.

I did my best to be available to Barb and Ben a couple times a day and tried to be present when hospice professionals were there. Sometimes they would call me to relay information Barbara found confusing. Ben was generally comfortable and his occasional delusions were, for the most part, joyful and sweet, as was his nature. The few tense moments when his attitude changed would upset Barbara. We worked through it with hospice support.

Just the day before Ben quietly died in the early morning hours, a hospice aide and I had bathed him and cut his hair. He had remarked how good he felt and even joked with me as I left that day. I felt good that the simple comfort of feeling clean relaxed him so he could leave on his terms. In this case, my aunt's stress was somewhat alleviated because Ben did not slip into a prolonged coma. He seemed alert on some level until it was time for him to cross over. Then he just went to sleep.

A DEATHBED RESOLUTION

We brought my husband's parents, Walt and Freda, to our town in 2007. Walt had been ill and in the hospital so we placed him in a nearby residential care home. Freda was clearly losing ground in cognitive abilities, but she was able to do much for herself. She moved in with us. A couple weeks later, Walt was again hospitalized and quickly lapsed into a coma. He was gone before Freda knew what was going on and her reaction was quite emotionally detached. I did my best to support her, though the onset of dementia made it unclear whether she actually grieved the loss of her spouse.

Freda's personality was one of contrasts: one moment girlish giggles, the next moment tantrums and biting words designed to hit her target's weakest spot. Through the years, her erratic personality had tested her son, Jim. He now wanted to do the right thing by his elderly parents, but I became the buffer when she treated him poorly. Throughout our relationship, Freda also attempted to push the limits of my patience and tolerance. This was curious to me, but I felt strongly the behavior was something rooted in her difficult childhood. Over time Freda revealed tragic memories of her youth that had clearly shaped her insecurities. Knowing this, I felt compassion for her.

Before and after she moved in, I had promised Freda I would always be honest with her. If she required more care than I could provide she would need to move to a care setting. Around the same time my Uncle Ben was in rapid decline, my mother-in-law began to require care that bordered on medical. One particular afternoon, Freda and I laughed about the predicament we found ourselves in and which neither of us was particularly happy about. I was doctor-designated to administer medication anally. Thanks to her blue sense of humor, I was able to tease Freda that I was finally going to "get even." We laughed and cooperatively got through the moment, but both of us knew it signaled a turning point.

After seeing Uncle Ben off for another hospital emergency, Freda told me the time had come for her to go to the care home. In addition to our medication predicament from the day before, she realized that my aunt and uncle were in a phase requiring more care and that I had very little time for my business clients and to be a wife to her son. I knew better than to delay making arrangements for her relocation. Bless Freda's heart for being the one to suggest what needed to happen. Despite her loss of independence in many things, she made sure she was in charge of that decision. She courageously made a decision most people avoid at all costs. I suspect it helped that she met some of the ladies living there during an earlier vacation stay. After the move, Freda would occasionally check in with me as to how her placement occurred.

"I made the decision to move myself, didn't I?" she would ask. I reassured her she absolutely did make the decision and that I appreciated her consideration of me in doing so. We were blessed that her care home was so close by that we saw her three or more times a week.

When Freda began her end-of-life process with hospice and she drifted in and out of sleep, she begged her mother out loud during a fitful daytime nap not to leave her behind. And she then called to her brother, also long deceased, to help her. I was surprised she was working to resolve lifelong emotional issues as she prepared to die, but the hospice nurse told me she had seen it before. This seemed proof to me she had begun visiting the other side during those deep sleep periods. She would awaken after a few minutes with no apparent memory of her dream.

Given that she demonstrated a challenging personality at times when she lived with us, it was especially touching when she began to "settle accounts" with me. "We're OK, right?" she queried one afternoon from the bed in her sunny room. "I mean, we are friends, aren't we?"

My assurance that we were indeed friends put a broad smile on her face. She seemed encouraged to pursue more assurance. "I made the decision to come here, right? I mean, I decided when it was time to move here, didn't I?"

"Yes, you did. And I was very grateful you made that decision because I was worried I would not be able to give you the nursing care you required," I replied. I continued as I saw the reinforcement was comforting to her. "I wanted you to be happy and I'm glad we could work together as a team to make sure you get what you need."

Soon Freda was asleep most of the time and then in a coma. The staff at the residential care facility took care of all her personal needs but California law did not allow staff to give her morphine to ease her breathing and assure her comfort. I was particularly moved at this time to see Jim become even more engaged in his mother's comfort and care. Their relationship had been tense at times through the years, but he clearly was eager to see that she was comfortable. In terms of caregiving, this was a simple but important job that he felt competent to do. Sometimes he would go alone to the care home to administer her morphine and spend time with her. Most times we would go together.

For about a week my husband and I visited her three times daily to administer her morphine that eased her breathing. The hospice care she received, along with the constant attention of the care home staff, gave my husband, his brother, Dennis, and me tremendous comfort. The three of us gathered at the care home on the afternoon of March 31 when we felt her transition was imminent. Her doctor stopped by the same day around 5:00 p.m. and spoke with her as she slept. We always waited for the pauses in her breathing pattern to end before stepping away from her bed to go home. And we always spoke to her assuming she could hear us. We left again on this day after telling Freda we would return that night at the usual time to administer her medications.

It was after 11:00 that night when we returned and joined the gentleman on staff who sat at her bedside. We visited and lingered, speaking softly among ourselves and to Freda. Soon after administering her liquid morphine inside her cheek, Jim told his mother that he loved her and that we would return in the morning if she still needed us. As we had done dozens of times, we waited for her breathing cycle to restart before leaving the room. Then we turned to exit.

"Wait. We can't go now. She's leaving," Jim said, turning back to his mother.

I put my handbag down and went to Freda, who appeared about the same. I took her bony wrist in my hand and felt her pulse. It was erratic and pounding wildly beneath her papery skin. And then it stopped. She was gone less than a minute after Jim had sensed her departure. I asked Jim how he knew she was leaving and he could not express why he knew. In that moment, it seemed to me something very special had happened, but I did not want to intrude too deeply into my husband's thoughts in the moments after his mother passed.

The next morning, Jim and I awoke and started our day very quietly. At this point, I could no longer resist checking in with him to see if he also recognized the amazing connection he'd made with his mother. Whenever we discussed spirituality, Jim tended to keep his thoughts brief while I loved to talk in detail about how we are all connected by something larger than ourselves.

"Honey, did you notice how after you told your mother that you loved her, she seemed to reach out to you without speaking to say goodbye?"

He thought for a few seconds before responding in the simple way that was his style during these discussions. "Well, it did occur to me that she was here for me when I came into this world and I was here for her when she left."

"Good enough," I thought. But I will never forget the wonder of witnessing that connection and their mutual healing of bad feelings over long-ago hurts. What a privilege to see that. It was also a gift to me that my husband seemed a bit lighter and easier going as the days passed. How much work Freda had done at the end! Such a lesson for me that death really is part of life.

It later occurred to me how fitting it was that Freda chose to leave on April Fool's Day. Despite her variable temperament, she loved to joke around and laugh, so I have no doubt she was quite proud of her very fitting departure date. Of course, I think of her every year and wonder if she will play a joke on me.

MOM'S DELIVERY FROM DEMENTIA

Over time, my mother's dementia brought an end to her independence. Because they lived closer, the burden for dealing with her needs lay largely on my brothers, Stuart and Stephen, but most especially on older Stuart. The three of us and my sister-in-law, Fran, worked together to relocate Mom to live near Stuart and Fran, an emotional and bonding time for us. Under Stuart's kind and judicious care, when it became obvious she needed to have still more care, he hired someone to help in her apartment and began making plans to place her in assisted living.

Her placement was imminent when Stuart and his wife, Fran, took a short trip together. On the day they were heading home, he called Mom to tell her he would be home shortly and that her caregiver would arrive within the hour. They had a pleasant conversation that concluded with "I love you." Our mother then died quietly in her chair, found by her caregiver within the hour.

Toward the end of her life, my mother was not very self-aware so far as we observed. It is possible some part of her subconscious was still on track. She had moments of lucidity and we wondered what came to her in those random and fleeting bursts of awareness that might have signaled it was time to leave. Though she was cognitively challenged, our mother was relatively healthy in a physical sense, including mobility. She was not a candidate for hospice. We weren't even considering the possibility of her death when it happened.

Stuart had broken the news to her of her impending placement in a facility, not entirely sure she comprehended what he was saying. Mom stated many times that she hoped to live as long and be as active as her older sister, whose death preceded hers by just five days. Had that sad news touched something in her? Her sudden death took us all by surprise and had an air of mystery that made it seem as though she made the decision about the timing of her transition. We just knew we were grateful Mom was spared some of the indignities of late-stage dementia.

It was also a blessing she had no other apparent forms of suffering. The consciousness has many levels. Perhaps, too, she was able to have whatever resolution she needed to be ready to cross over. Regardless, if she was ready to move on, I could accept that.

DISCUSSING MORTALITY IS NOT MORBID

Along with senior family members, the loss of numerous friends near our age gave Jim and me many reasons to discuss death and dying before he received his terminal diagnosis. We talked about how calm my friend Jan was, having accepted her terminal cancer diagnosis after several bouts and battles. We considered how my father had taken treatment until very near the end of his life for my mother's sake, and what we felt they lost in terms of time to say important things to each other. Knowing Mom was in denial about Dad's terminal status, I felt they both missed out on some precious moments of tenderness as she busied herself with housework in order to not think about losing him.

Our personal experiences with family deaths reshaped our thinking and ideas about dying. Jim, in particular, went from making statements such as "If I ever get that way, promise you will shoot me" to talking about the amazing work hospice did for his family, and even telling friends. For a guy who could be quiet when it came to heavy discussions, death and hospice no longer seemed to be taboo or macabre because he witnessed how hospice can normalize that phase of life. It did not seem that he had become desensitized to dying by being exposed to it, but rather that he was sensitized to accept what the process of dying could bring to everyone who cared to pay attention.

CHAPTER SUMMARY

- It is often received as good news by hospice patients that most humans die gently in their sleep.
- When difficult questions are answered, some dying patients can better focus on living their final days.
- The time when patients drift in and out of consciousness or when they are in a coma before death can be a highly productive time when they resolve hurts and past concerns before the final transition. Conversely, the act of caring for or observing the death of a loved one during this time can be healing, even life-changing, for others.
- Fear of death or loss is often at the core of denial and unwillingness to plan for one's death.
- Many family members who are not ready to let go of a loved one believe it is loving to continue treatment beyond its benefit or to artificially and futilely extend a dying person's life. Religious beliefs can also play a part in these decisions.
- Dignified hospice care is often a factor in helping patients feel prepared to ease into death.
- There can be profound and inexplicable connections between the dying and loved ones.
- Occasionally, an older adult will seem able to let go of this life and move on as if by a simple decision, while most others take longer to balance body, mind, and spirit in order to be at peace with dying.

- Thinking of the natural death process as part of life helps facilitate conversation and normalizes the experience of being around the dying patient.
- Those closest to the dying can make decisions as to what would make their loved one most comfortable during the transition to death, such as whether to stay at their bedside or leave the room. The right way is what seems right for the individuals involved who know each other best.

Resources

www.caregiver.org/guide-to-understanding-dementia-behaviors

Printable guide to handling dementia behaviors

"Gone from my Sight" by Barbara Karnes, RN: www.bkbooks.com

Site allows purchase of booklet describing body changes approaching final months, weeks, and days until death.

Chapter Two

PLANNING AHEAD

GROWING OLD IS A PRIVILEGE
DENIED TO MANY

If you are a role model, or an artistic or generous or thoughtful or spiritual person, how you die can be a reflection of the best parts of you. A well thought-out plan for the all-important end-time of your life that eases your suffering will leave loved ones with positive feelings that go a long way toward overcoming their grief. Your good planning and acceptance frees them to focus on the blessings of special moments toward the end of your life. And you will have left something very meaningful for them—a sense of your ongoing influence on and presence in their lives.

Since you have picked up this book, you have likely given some thought to or had ideas about the issues that arise for the dying and their families, so we will now switch gears to look at your options for the future. Having read the first chapter, you now have some sense that end of life is a very dynamic time for the person who is actively transitioning. It is an important phase of life and worthy of careful planning that can also help those who love you. If you know what you *don't* want at that time, you can exercise control by putting your wishes in writing and removing the guesswork for those who will carry out your wishes. As difficult as death can be to think about, try to think of how you die as being an important part of how you live.

It is unknown where he first heard it, but my husband had a favorite saying for his friends who complained about the aches and inconveniences of aging. Jim would always reply, "Growing old is a privilege denied to many." Jim's death, coming at age seventy, seemed early to me. I don't necessarily feel he lived to what I think of as old age, but perhaps that is because I am not that far from seventy myself. I will say, once he knew there was a specific expiration date, Jim made the most of the time he had; you'll read more about that in a bit.

Should you think you will save time by skipping this section of the book because planning is boring or because you have already made all the end-of-life plans you need to make, please note there are some aspects of planning covered in here you have probably have never considered. In the event of a sudden death, financial planning (a will and trust, for example) is a wonderful thing to have in place. It is important to know your family will be taken care of when you are gone and to spell out the distribution of assets. There are many experts to consult on those matters and we urge you to make time in your busy life to do so sooner rather than later. However, this book is first and foremost about you and what you want and need for a peaceful end. Secondarily, it is about informing those around you of your needs and wishes and helping familiarize them with what will be involved.

None of us is assured a long life. Each day lives end suddenly for many reasons, natural and unnatural. For that reason alone, we should all be motivated to do some end-of-life planning for our families. In the case of a sudden death of a loved one, families are thrown into a turmoil of grief and bewilderment at the sudden loss. When the deceased has not completed an end-of-life document, they can be thrown into financial and emotional chaos as well. Failure of the deceased to have an accessible plan often creates ill-will among family members who assume they know what the deceased would have wanted. Some families include members whose behavior challenges the others during difficult times. Without a written plan, a determined person could challenge and succeed at changing the oral plan between spouses, for instance. So I would urge you to pursue a written plan now, as though your time could end this year without warning.

It isn't that adults are all averse to planning, but it is end-of-life planning that is most avoided. After all, many spend a great deal of time and energy on retirement planning from a financial standpoint. Many adults also address changes that are matters of convenience, rather than accommodation. One example is the vast numbers of older adults who downsize their homes or change to single-story residences for their physical convenience or smaller homes for financial flexibility. But most will stop short of initiating planning for end of life because it is an uncomfortable subject.

I have heard middle-aged adults say they are delaying end-of-life planning because they expect "things will change" and, yes, documents will need to be updated. Put it on your calendar to review your important end-of-life papers annually. Checking in with your estate planning attorney every few years can save money down the line. Not only will changes in your own health affect your wishes, you will quickly realize how a wedding, birth, reversal of circumstances, or retirement can become important to your planning. Make it your goal to keep your end-of-life plan up to date.

I have said and will continue to say, there were many, many more moments of joy and gratitude made possible during the two years following my husband's terminal diagnosis because Jim chose to live his life fully. Additionally, he made a lifelong habit of saving and planning for his retirement and our future, and he continued planning following his diagnosis. His good efforts in that regard have given his family much to be grateful for in terms of our financial security. He did confide to me that it was a source of personal pride that he was able to provide meaningfully for us even though he had earned a modest living all his life. However, it was Jim's willingness to confront the decisions that made his end of life more manageable that contributed to his sense of peace, as well as provided us with more blessings than I can count.

There is nothing worse than seeing a loved one suffer needlessly. Jim thanked me on numerous occasions during his final weeks for caring for him, but all thanks were owed to him. Knowing that his final weeks on earth were as gentle and peaceful as possible was of tremendous comfort to me. I could not have done for him what I did (with hospice support, of course) if he had been resistant to allowing the proper resources we had planned for to come into play when needed. I am confident Jim's openness to discussing and allowing end-of-life planning made his transition easier and it left me with more moments of gratitude to contemplate. I am convinced that planning for his end of life made my healing easier and this is an important reason why I encourage you to take the time to think about planning for your end of life.

PLANNING TO DIE AT HOME

Most people died at home until the mid-twentieth century. Often several generations of family lived together caring for the young, the sick, and the dying at home, which exposed all generations to this expected, final mortal event. This is still the case in many parts of the world. However, over time in the United States and now in our modern era, death has become secretive, taboo, mostly hidden away in hospitals.

In the late 1960s and early 1970s the human potential and home birth movements were gaining ground in popularity in the United States. Around the same time, Elizabeth Kubler-Ross started a death-awareness movement to encourage Americans to consider death as a natural and dignified final chapter of life. Five years after her book about dying, On Death & Dying *(1969), was published, the first hospice opened in the United States. Today, hospice care in one's home is gaining acceptance. Slowly, Americans have been opening up again to natural approaches to life and death. However, resistance and misinformation continue to inhibit and delay entry into hospice.*

As you prepare end-of-life documents, you will want to consider where you want to spend your final days. According to Centers for Disease Control, despite the fact that more than 80 percent of Medicare beneficiaries aged sixty-five and older wanted to die at home, in 2013 one third, about 1.9 million deaths among that group, occurred in the hospital, about the same proportion as in the previous twelve years. There are many reasons for this discrepancy, including lack of knowledge about care options, lack of a well-informed, written plan for the end of one's life, financial considerations, and fear of death. Creating a health care directive requires an understanding of different systems of health care for the end of life, including palliative care and hospice.

Hospice is a system of visiting professionals who provide emotional and spiritual care to the client and family members while managing the terminal patient's pain and other physical symptoms. Hospice organizations do not represent any specific religious belief but support and respect the beliefs of their clients. There are hospice organizations in all states but some remote areas may not have access. It behooves these individuals to inquire where they might receive hospice services in a facility. For more information about hospice, go to www.caringinfo.org

Medicare recipients are covered for hospice care, as are most other insured individuals. Most hospice organizations accept insurances and many provide care to the uninsured. Most hospice organizations accept clients when they are within six months of dying. These clients, in most areas (whether receiving care at home or in a hospice facility), can receive this care if two physicians certify that they qualify. Generally, they must re-qualify (be assessed as to meeting Medicare eligibility requirements) every three months for the first six months. Thereafter re-qualifying is done every two months. On occasion, a hospice client will have a period of stable health or remission that allows them to be temporarily discharged from hospice until decline becomes apparent once again.

Palliative care is an option if one has a terminal or serious disease and wishes to receive possibly curative or life-extending treatments while receiving assertive symptom management, such as for nausea and vomiting caused by cancer treatment. Before making treatment choices, a palliative care consult for assistance with and advocacy for quality symptom and pain management helps to steer one through the many options in the health care system to make informed decisions for treatment. Each decision has to be evaluated to assess burdens and benefits of the treatment. Another way of assessing this is to ask whether quality of life will be improved or further compromised with the treatment. A palliative care professional will check in with the patient to make sure at each step of the way that treatment is achieving the patient's goals. For more information on this option, visit www.getpalliativecare.org.

Planning for the end of life is essential. You are effectively planning how your body will be treated and cared for by others while you are living and until you die. Without a plan, the health care system often utilizes aggressive and invasive treatments to prolong life. Others will be burdened with making decisions that may not align with your choices, values, and beliefs. Once your plans are written and communicated you can have peace of mind, reduce or eliminate family conflicts, and minimize stress over your care. For general information on this topic of advanced health care planning, or if dementia is a concern, visit www.caringinfo.org.

There is good news that there is no evidence of any connection between crafting one's advance health care directives and increasing your risk of earlier death. And, though some may fear that allowing life to follow a natural course to its end means a loss of control, planning for it and understanding the processes is helpful in restoring a sense of calm and control of one's own agenda for the remainder of life.

PLANNING IS A LOVING THING TO DO

It can be a matter of pride and a source of comfort to have one's own end-of-life planning in place. It certainly was that to my husband. Making your own end-of-life plan can also make it easier to discuss the matter with your parents and to possibly assist them in making their own plan. If your parents resist making plans or refuse to use helpful resources as they age, you may be in a position only to observe and then deal with what I would describe as "work-arounds." Any experience in the preparation or helping aspects of end of life is very likely to reinforce your resolve to do a better job planning for your own end of life.

The recently released book *Modern Death: How Medicine Changed the End of Life* makes an elegant case for each of us taking personal responsibility to understand issues surrounding end of life. The author, Haider Warraich, MD, points out how planning ahead benefits all involved and says there is evidence that individuals with spouses are most likely to have their final wishes closely followed.

Jim's children were independent adults when we became a couple. He was nearly a decade older, so we always talked about what he wanted to do for his daughters financially when he passed. I never wanted to quibble with family members over money and other issues, so his direction and guidance were appreciated by me. It also signaled his love and trust that I would follow his wishes, something very important to me as his life partner. As I was not the mother of his children, it seemed prudent that Jim's wishes for distribution of his assets were discussed many times and understood by me from the start.

For me, importance also needed to be placed on matters such as funeral preparations and placement of his remains. Since it was his choice for me to oversee the arrangements, I wanted Jim to put every detail in writing. I had seen too many conflicts in blended families when various family members had differing ideas about what should happen. Death brings to the forefront raw emotion and unexpected conflict. I have often felt that is due to fear but have learned that self-serving motives and projecting one's own feelings and wishes onto someone else frequently figures into the dysfunction equation. Everyone thinks they know what the dying or deceased would want, but the only way to be sure is for the individual to put everything in writing in advance so their wishes can be honored.

Some may disagree, but I would also say that there cannot be too much detail in one's funeral planning. A disagreement over something as simple as what the deceased should wear can be the beginning of resentments that reverberate through the family for years. My suggestion is that everyone decide right down to the necktie how they want to be presented for burial, or what they want to be wearing (if anything) when they are cremated or buried. Discuss these details with the mortuary or contracting service when making arrangements. Choose a service with nationwide affiliates so your wishes can be easily carried out and your pre-arranged payments will be honored even if you relocate before dying. There may be some small local fees or items not covered in the burial insurance plan, but the bulk of the cost and arrangements will be in place so things can proceed smoothly.

Like most couples, Jim and I thought there was plenty of time for lawyers and planning in our future. My husband was not yet sixty-nine years old when we received word of his terminal illness. I thought we would have another ten to fifteen years before his health began to significantly decline, so there was much left to put into writing once we learned the gravity of his illness.

As soon as we absorbed the news of his impending death, Jim made appointments with his financial planner and an attorney to complete his distribution of assets planning. I understand this may not be the way everyone responds to news of their terminal diagnosis, but it was always Jim's style to take care of business immediately, especially since he still felt strong and capable. He also went to the funeral home alone to make those arrangements. Jim probably felt more comfortable addressing his funeral planning with the funeral home director, a man of tremendous compassion. I understood Jim was still grappling with these new and upsetting developments, so it wouldn't have been helpful for me to join him.

Once the paperwork was completed and signed, Jim shared the plans with his daughters so they would know in advance that the planning was his choice and that he had designated me to carry out his wishes. Jim was fortunate to have respectful daughters who would not challenge his choices, but we know this is not the case for all families. I think his sharing the information before he died took all the surprises and any big disappointments out of the equation. It also assured that the rituals surrounding his passing would not be marred with hard feelings. That is why I say planning and making known the plan to those involved is the loving thing to do.

PUT YOUR PLAN IN WRITING

The necessity of a well-written advanced health care directive *that is not only written but discussed with loved ones cannot be over-stated. In cases of a dementia diagnosis, a videotaped description of one's wishes should be recorded as soon as possible while one still has legal (mental) capacity. An advanced directive is a legal document that directs your agent (usually a spouse or family member) to follow steps you have outlined regarding life-saving or comfort care choices. It directs your health care agent (the person you have named to make decisions on your behalf when you can no longer do so) as to what steps to take to save your life and what measures you do not want taken. Therefore, it is imperative that the person(s) responsible for executing your wishes know where and how to access this directive. Online access and special cell phone apps are being developed for this purpose and deserve consideration. Web registries are one proposed manner of storing advance-planning documents online, including advance health care directives, making it possible for the information to be available to different providers in any location. Still in the development stages as of 2017, it remains to be seen if this will become a viable tool.*

It should be noted here that even legal documents are challenged. This is especially true if there is rivalry or discord among family members. Most often, but not always, a capable spouse is the one chosen to support and execute end-of-life and post-mortem wishes. Those without a spouse should take all precautions and legally designate a decision-maker in writing. Failure to do so leaves a door open to those who are more interested in their own needs than yours, including dysfunctional children and more distant relatives.

Writing one's health care directive is also necessary because of the way modern Western medicine is practiced. Therefore, the burden is on the users of the health care system to make known their wishes if they want to limit the care they receive. Our current fee-for-service health care system is supported by maximizing the treatment of individuals. It is also vital to take this planning step because death so often does not take place at home, where it is most desired and where it can be most personalized. Even young people are advised to do this because the risk of accidental severe and debilitating injury or death is so high among that group. If you are severely injured and not expected to fully recover, medical practitioners will keep you alive unless they have a directive from you to do otherwise. Many people live with certain limitations and disabilities, but you may specify which living conditions, for you, would be worse than death.

If your desire is to die at home, include in your directive that you do not wish to die in a hospital where you are likely to be subjected to constant audible alarms, noises of activity, periodic blood draws and vital signs night and day. Privacy and quiet are indispensable to a dignified end and are typically in short supply in a hospital unless there is a hospice wing.

WRITTEN DIRECTIVES CAN
REDUCE SUFFERING

Studies published in the Journal of the American Osteopathic Association (July 2006, Vol. 106, 402-404) show elderly adults hold often erroneous and overly-optimistic beliefs about successful outcomes of CPR. When an unconscious patient in a health crisis arrives at a hospital without a written advance health care directive, if CPR has been successful, the person will be transferred to the ICU. The ICU is a highly technical setting without privacy for the patient who must be constantly monitored. It is not a setting for a calm, quietly contemplative end. If the unconscious person does not awaken, the health team must consult with the family as to any desires expressed by the patient for further care or life-extending measures. Until a friend or family member is consulted, life-saving protocols will be followed by the medical professionals managing the case.

The following information regarding CPR and intubation is graphic and may be alarming to some, but I feel it is better to have the knowledge and make an informed choice in advance than to live these circumstances against your will. To help you have a clear picture as to what CPR involves, the following procedures are common practice absent breathing and/or heartbeat:

- *Absent independent breathing and/or heartbeat, create an airway (intubation) by inserting a plastic tube about one-inch wide down trachea (windpipe)*
- *Establish an IV line by placing a needle followed by a plastic tube into a vein*
- *Perform chest compressions (100 per minute) by vigorously depressing the sternum approximately two to two-and-a-half inches*
- *If a heartbeat is not restarted by compressions, electrical shock may be applied to the chest*

Compression and electrical shock is repeated indefinitely until resuscitation, until a doctor decides to stop, or as prescribed by rescue protocol, which is determined by the agency or medical organization providing service. Some of these procedures are likely to cause injury, including broken bones, especially in the elderly. A study in the Journal of Osteopathic Association, 7/2006, Vol. 106, 402-404, *showed rates of survival from CPR actually range from 3.8 percent to 17.1 percent for the elderly. At best, for those over age seventy, less than 20 percent will survive CPR to leave the hospital. It is essential to be well informed and realistic when considering CPR, especially if you are elderly and infirm, since elders are not likely to survive this intensely invasive set of actions in and on your body.*

I have witnessed patients who died after being intubated for many days. Intubation is accomplished with a firm plastic tube sitting in the mouth and down the throat, taped in place. It is a painful, invasive method for providing oxygen when the person cannot breathe without help. It is a challenge to manage a patient's anxiety and discomfort due to the tube extending into their trachea. Health care personnel and loved ones alike find it difficult to watch someone who is aware of the tube as they struggle against it. If you choose to receive CPR, you are also choosing intubation if you are not breathing on your own.

If the patient never verbalized any choices about health care, such as wanting or not wanting to live indefinitely while critically ill, the family would be asked to decide on the patient's behalf. Many families cannot reach consensus on minor issues, let alone such vital ethical matters as turning off a ventilator. In these cases, the hospital health care team would most likely meet with their ethics committee to assist in decision making along with meeting with family members to reach an ethically sound decision. In summary, if you remain unconscious without a written health directive, other people will decide what happens to your body, and your body may receive multiple invasive, painful procedures during the remainder of your life.

One case of mine that is sadly commonplace was that of an elderly man in the last stage of dementia. He was nonverbal, unable to swallow, and his joints were so contracted that he appeared painfully twisted. He was extremely thin and nearing death but had neglected to write down or tell his family his end-of-life wishes before his dementia advanced. The nursing home team went along with his daughter's wishes to keep him alive as long as possible by feeding him liquid food through a stomach tube. He qualified for hospice, so I became his nurse, observing how he grimaced whenever he was turned in bed. I saw how he coughed and spit up excess secretions from the tube feedings his body did not tolerate well. In order to spare this patient an uncomfortable death from respiratory distress caused by excess secretions, I advocated for him to be given pain medicine and for the feedings to slow down, which the daughter declined due to her personal beliefs. I watched this suffering man and vowed I would spread the word of the vital, critical necessity of preparing a written personal health directive.

Whatever your choices, keep in mind that having the assistance of an attorney in crafting your personal end-of-life plan can provide added assurance that your decisions will be clear and enforceable.

THE ADDED CONSIDERATION OF DEMENTIA

Dementia care in the United States is bankrupting families and our health care system. According to the National Alzheimer's Association, one in three seniors now die with dementia, and this percentage is growing with Baby Boomers. It is the single disease of the top ten US causes of death that currently has no prevention or cure options. It is essential to consider possible complications of *dementia when planning for one's advanced health care directive. We cannot know the amount of suffering endured by demented persons. Nor can we guess what their choice would have been if the onset of dementia arrived before a choice was expressed. But you readers have a choice and I feel compelled to explain why making an advance decision about your care can be beneficial.*

There are millions of bed-bound patients in facilities who have advanced dementia and are no longer capable of communication, self-feeding, or self-care of any kind. Symptoms and processes vary widely among the multiple types of dementia and multiple courses the condition can take. There is evidence some dementias tend to run in families. Becoming familiar with the different forms of dementia can help when planning one's advanced health directive. Published material available on this topic is listed in the "Resources" section at the end of this chapter. It is common for dementia patients to live many years after they have lost all abilities for self-care, mobility, and communication. Therefore, one needs to consider how long and at what level of incapacity one wishes to live.

Deciding the most humane options for dementia clients is a contentious ethical concern for all of us to consider. When one develops one's health directive, it can and should be very specific, addressing common health challenges and outcomes such as ceasing intake of food and fluids. With the prediction that 45 percent of eighty-five-year-olds will have dementia, it is wise to write (and videotape) one's plan prior to onset of dementia. That said, as I write this you should know that making plans while of sound mind to foreshorten your life as a demented patient has not been tested in all state courts and may not be an option if the patient is in a licensed nursing home.

How you wish to be treated if you become demented is a question for you to answer and put in place long before you have any inkling whether you will become a dementia patient. You may be on a physical track to last to age eighty-five or longer, but if you become severely demented by age eighty, what would you want? Would it be better for you to pass away peacefully much sooner, or would you prefer to be kept clinically alive? Would you want your family or health care agent to insist you are tube fed when you can no longer swallow? If you do not make your decision beforehand and put it in writing, your family is likely to keep you alive until your heart stops. If dementia and expert care planning are concerns for you and your family, visit the website www.caringadvocates.org.

It should be noted that the impact on loved ones who witness the debilitating decline and prolonged discomforts of a loved one, as well as bearing the financial responsibility for care, can be devastating in the event of a lengthy course of dementia. I have had clients that have lived with dementia for fifteen years. That is a long time to visit the skilled nursing facility and bring supplies and medicines that are not provided. I recommend that you plan as though dementia is a possibility in your future so that you have choices to limit your suffering and that of your family.

PLAN FOR YOUR OWN INFIRMITY

No one has a view of the future nor do we typically possess advance knowledge as to how our lives will play out. Frailty is something we may think of as a very slow decline, but that is not always the case. Strokes and other catastrophic health episodes can render us infirm and dependent at once and may later contribute to death. Both Jo and I know of individuals who were placed in the hospital for sudden major health problems. While resting in the hospital, their family or friends step in to manage their home, pet, or garden. Then, after a time the doctor determines the individual cannot return home permanently or independently. What a shock to learn you will now be completely dependent and your entire life is changed. At least it would be of some small comfort to have a plan in place to inform reliable chosen persons how to act on your wishes.

For those who are of extremely limited income, who use programs of the state for support, it is important to have all your information and financial records in easily accessible order. You may be receiving Medicare, however you may need to quickly sign up for Medicaid if your health needs change and you require help to remain independent at home. The only place to receive twenty-four-hour physical help for an impoverished senior on Medicaid is in a nursing home.

The older we are, even if essentially healthy, the less able we are to handle huge transactions with ease. Even if fit and functioning, age ninety is very late to take on some of life's big tasks. These include the sale of a home, moving, re-homing a pet, or selecting a new living environment; and they often all happen at once. As they age, many adults become resistant to practical changes to make life less complicated, so it is better that one plan ahead and specify the circumstances that will initiate such transactions with help from trusted sources. Advance planning will guide those acting on your behalf and at least relieve you of additional stress beyond the changes to your life, especially if those changes are forced on you suddenly. Jo and I both recommend that all of us should look at late-life decisions logically and dispassionately well in advance. Doing so makes for better decisions than when we must respond to an emergency.

FINANCING LATE-LIFE CARE

Aging is a slow process. For most adults, the body weakens slowly from mid-life forward and we often require some help with activities of daily living. As stamina and stability diminish, fear of falling increases and adults become less inclined to venture far from home. For that reason, your planning now should include choices of where and how you want to live late in life, and how you can afford your chosen living arrangement.

Yes, I love my home, too. Though I've already set myself up in a single-story residence, there will likely come a time when a smaller home will be more suited to my needs and ability to care for myself. I want to be mentally prepared to let go when this house no longer works for me. I can look around and see the physical challenges in my home that might become problematic as I age. Therefore, it seems to me the willingness to prepare (ahead of the actual need) makes it easier to accept life on the terms that are presented. Willingness to adapt is part of being more satisfied and content in late life. Life is good now, but it is going to change. I want to be ready for that so I can continue to make the most of my days.

Down-sizing: After making an honest pros-and-cons list about aging in place, I suggest thinking about a timeline for selling your large family home before the need is immediate (and before you are frail and less able to deal with the transaction). In my case, for example, I already live in a relatively small single-story home designed so a wheelchair can be accommodated. I have built a large shower I can sit in. I have done so in a way that is decoratively attractive and does not make my home look as though it is retrofitted for solely senior occupants. I have added solar panels to reduce the electric bills and a water-saving device—both to help with my fixed retirement budget. I am gradually converting the yard to lower maintenance. I live in a family neighborhood, so I want lots of future buyers to see themselves being able to enjoy this house when I am ready to sell it.

If you are planning ahead and are fortunate enough to have the financial resources, it also pays to do things to make your home more valuable and to take advantage of those benefits while you live in the home. I expect to probably sell my home in my seventies, but possibly sooner. By investing now in improvements and maintenance, I am able to enjoy them and expect to be in a position for a quick sale when I feel the property is too much for me to handle or if something happens that requires me to make a sudden change. The cash from my equity will go a long way toward any specialized care I might need late in life or at the end of my life. Better yet, if I downsize while still relatively active and before poor health alters my lifestyle, I should be able to enjoy a few nice trips with friends from the proceeds of the home sale.

Reverse mortgage: An option used by many aging adults of limited income and assets to afford late-life care has been the reverse mortgage. This is a loan against a percentage of the equity in your home. The best situation is to have adequate wealth and income to afford the lifestyle and care choices you prefer. However, many older Americans live in poverty or on very limited incomes, relying only on Social Security. There are some legitimate reverse mortgage programs, but one must be astute to understand their details. If you want to look into a reverse mortgage, I suggest getting assistance from a financial adviser not connected with the reverse mortgage company.

Nationally renowned financial advice personality Suze Orman has reservations about reverse mortgages. In one of her articles on the CNBC website about the risks and rewards of reverse mortgages, she says, "I think reverse mortgages are a potentially dangerous step for many retirees . . . It is far too easy to get blinded by the prospect of receiving much-needed income today and overlook some important consideration . . . My recommendation is that you think of a reverse mortgage as a last resort emergency fund in retirement."

If your regular mortgage is not paid off or if the home doesn't pass the lender's inspection criteria, you may be ineligible for this option, anyway. Being personally aware of senior adults who did not understand their reverse mortgage programs and lenders who did not go out of their way to look out for the borrower, this is not an option I would recommend to a friend or loved one unless they have someone truly knowledgeable to look out for their best interests. For example, I know of one person who nearly lost her home to the reverse mortgage lender because she was unable to pay ongoing fees and insurance costs that she had not anticipated. Also, you need to review any reverse mortgage contract carefully to make sure your heirs will not be held responsible if the house decreases in value or for other fees.

A reverse mortgage may offer the benefit of allowing one to "age in place," however, that might not be desirable if the home is in poor condition or too challenging for an aging person to manage. It is important to age in the right place. Isolation is a key aspect of aging in place that should be of concern. I personally know a woman who took out a reverse mortgage on an extremely dilapidated home in an isolated area. She was approaching the age of 100 and living alone. There was much more to the story, but efforts were made to help this person. Sadly, she was no longer capable of good decisions and it was difficult to prove the bank had failed legally or morally in its role when they acted on their client's requests. Very old adults often stand in the way of changes and choices that would give them a happier and better life. At the same time, relatives and others may not always have their best interests in mind. Being of sound mind when the decisions are made and having someone in place to help facilitate one's wishes can prevent these problems. The Department of Housing and Urban Development website offers consumer information on reverse mortgages at www.hud.gov.

Long-term health care insurance: In this case, one pays premiums on an insurance policy to cover future health care needs. This wide-ranging subject must be thoroughly researched and carefully analyzed before choosing a plan. Ideally the chosen plan's provisions will cover the end-of-life options desired by the insured, including caregiver assistance when on hospice.

Long-term care insurance is an expensive option based on "educated guesses" (actuarial predictions) as to what your health and needs will be in the future. Seek a financial planner with fiduciary responsibilities and who has no connection with the long-term health care insurance industry for advice as to how effective this option would be for you. Be advised that plans can fail. As recently as April 2017, the *New York Times* reported the demise of Penn Treaty, based in Allentown, PA. The company's insureds had hoped to protect their families from overwhelming costs of late-life care. According to the article, Consumer Federation of America has been warning about problems with long-term care since the 1990s. After all, what tools do consumers have for evaluating the risk of any long-term care insurance company, especially when the time lapse between purchase and need can be so long?

On a personal note, there was a time I thought long-term care insurance would be my best option. I have no immediate family living in the area that I could lean on for a bit of extra help as I age. Jim was opposed to this due to the cost and uncertainty of its usefulness when the need arose. As it turns out, he knew my situation would be such that I would have the assets and savings to afford assisted living or additional care for some time when considering my finances and the equity in my home. This is a more appealing option to me as I can actually see what I have to work with and can make the adjustments in my own time rather than waiting for frailty and/or an emergency to trigger my care coverage under a long-term care plan.

Jo also pointed out to me there are waiting periods on some long-term care plans to begin receiving benefits, which can be financially challenging should assistance be needed immediately. Understand it is the insurer's decision when they will pay and the paperwork can be complicated and extensive to initiate payment. My preference would be to sell my home and have the proceeds under my control to care for myself.

Create added income or reduce expenses: Like television's *Golden Girls,* another way to afford to stay in one's own home or to have assistance at home is to take in a roommate or two. Any individual considered to live in the home should be well known to the homeowner with similar interests and (if possible) a little stronger and less frail. (Please do not go online and solicit strangers for this purpose.) The senior adult can charge a modest rent to a friend who provides social interaction and may be willing to drive them to doctor's appointments or to contact their family if more help is needed. If they are close in age they will enjoy dining out and going to the movies together and helping each other with things like laundry and shopping.

We are talking about an agreement between friends to be roommates, not trading room and board for services. I actually know small groups of women who discuss finding a space to live together and support one another. This is a good option for women, who tend to live longer and to be more social with their friends than men. However, it requires planning and discussion long before the need arises. My friends and I are already talking about it, but we also know that agreements of this type need to be put in writing and signed.

WHEN FAMILY IS FAR AWAY

Hiring caregivers: Many adults who live to advanced age will require the assistance of a caregiver at some point in time. Chapter 5 will deal with more specifics about providing and receiving care. This section relates to knowing in advance what care options are available in your area and how you would like to utilize them if and when the need arises.

If you do not have family or friends nearby who can periodically assist, and if the need becomes more than occasional, hired caregivers are the answer. These workers may perform housework, cook meals, or do any myriad of home-making and personal care chores. They may take the elder to the doctor or provide personal care and socialization. Depending on the need, these home workers may work a few hours a week to full-time, round-the-clock, even residing in the residence.

If hired directly by the elder, these workers become employees of the person receiving care. When you are looking into the implications of hiring home care workers for the first time, expect that you should keep records and report activity on your federal tax filing. This can be a burdensome task for someone who is not in good health. Therefore, many hire and pay workers under the table, which we cannot encourage. Workers can quit or fail to show up and leave the elder unattended. There are also potential tax liabilities, as well as insurance liabilities if a worker creates problems.

As for live-in workers, it can be done well privately, most often if there is a family member or someone to oversee that they are performing well and not taking advantage. Unfortunately, when a frail senior is isolated in the home with a caregiver, abuses can occur if their care is not monitored. There is an added complication if a live-in worker has to be let go because they are both a tenant and a worker in some jurisdictions. Think of the implications and difficulties of trying to evict someone who is being replaced for neglecting their senior employer. That is why I like the idea of multiple workers who do not live in full-time. There are back-ups if someone is sick or when a vacation is needed. When the worker has their own home, they have separation from the job for a private life, which is healthy for everyone.

Check in your community through friends, at senior centers and churches, and through the local health care system for professional home care agencies. Though costlier, advantages to having workers through an agency are several. The agency keeps the records and handles the taxes. You also have recourse if someone is not doing the job as you would like. You just call for a replacement, or you use another agency.

Planning for home maintenance and pets: Jo has told me of clients who are suddenly and unexpectedly in health crises and remanded to skilled nursing or some other care setting after hospitalization, never to return home or see their pets again. One may hope to return home but, sadly, it is not unusual for a health change or sudden onset of decline to cause an individual to be suddenly and permanently placed in a care setting. This is one of the saddest circumstances to have to plan for, but it can happen to anyone. It seems to me it would be better to have a plan in place than to add worry over what to do on top of the anguish and grief of loss.

Everyone should have a plan in the form of a simple call list for making sure these matters are not overlooked. Even if nobody will occupy the home for the short-term, you want to be sure the landscape is maintained and that the house is secure. This includes removing food that can spoil and cleaning the home if not left in good order. A trusted family member or professional should remove valuables and secure items such as the computer and paperwork until you or your personal representative can dispense with them according to your wishes. If or when it becomes time to sell the residence or other property you can use the proceeds to finance the lifestyle you want in old age. A trusted professional who has this information well before it is needed will relieve you of some stress in times of change by keeping you informed and reassured.

Most people don't think of their pets as property because they are truly part of the family. It is as hard to think about giving away my Chihuahua, Lily-Lou, as it is for me to think of her dying, but it is not an option for me to leave her adrift should something happen to me during her lifetime. If you have not done so, please make arrangements for someone who knows and loves your pet to look out for them or place them should you become unable to keep them. In my case, I have two dear friends who will work together to look after my dog's immediate needs and to find a good home placement that will match her temperament. Both have spent lots of time with her and are familiar with her behavior. As sad as the idea of placing her or not seeing her again is to me, I feel I have done right by her to pre-plan her future. In fact, on the next update of my trust, I will include an amount of money to care for her for a year or two. I think this is a good idea because she is likely to be placed with an older adult who might be on a limited income and I want to open up the adoption process to include those who could really appreciate Lil for her best qualities.

Professional care coordination: Private geriatric care managers can act as surrogate family members for someone whose abilities are diminished. They are licensed, most often as clinical social workers, and will help assist in identifying needs and solutions for most aspects of a client's life. They hire caregivers and help supervise them. They may also call a plumber when needed and make sure the bills are paid on time, most often by agreement of the person needing care and family members. If the client has the means and if it is practical to keep them in their home, the private care manager may supervise accommodations, such as having ramps built for wheelchairs and installing or ordering adaptive equipment as appropriate to assist the client. For clients who are financially "well off," a bank trust officer may hire such a care professional at the request of their client.

Being an individual whose family is located at various points across the United States, it has occurred to me that I may require the services of a professional to look out for my financial and overall well-being, especially if I begin to show signs of dementia. I have seen how challenging (often impossible) it can be for an older adult of diminishing capacity to look after a checking account or to call a refrigerator repair service. They put off decisions when they don't feel well and neglect can cost them more money than a limited income can withstand.

Having someone knowledgeable designated to make decisions when you are unwell or of diminished capacity is important. This can be an attorney or professional fiduciary if you don't have a trusted family member or friend. There can be many reasons to involve a professional, private fiduciary. Blended families and distrust between family members are also common reasons that individuals seek an impartial individual to handle their affairs. It should be noted that a professional private fiduciary, like an attorney or financial adviser, is held to a higher standard than family or friends.

Having an attorney and a private fiduciary to look out for my interests when I am unable to do so will not only help me live better, but will relieve my long-distance family members of worry. Again, I don't know exactly where I will live when I am older. I might be interested in relocating to be near family, but my current thought is to be near my friends I have grown old with.

Either way, having someone who can visit me and who is pre-authorized to have my roof leak repaired or to assure that my physicians have good information about my current status, as well as to oversee my placement in a care environment, will relieve a huge burden from me and help protect my assets. Many states have associations of private fiduciaries or guardians. In California, for instance, www.pfac-pro.org is the web link I highly recommend you investigate this option, including a meeting with one or two qualified professionals in your area.

It will help you adjust later on if you have looked into all the scenarios before you latch onto one plan and assume you will be able to or must stay with it. Being educated about the options and watching elders and friends go through their aging process can help you adjust to the array of options that may suit your changing needs as you age. Think living well as you age rather than trying to live forever as you lived at age forty or fifty.

CONSIDERATION FOR FEARS OF DYING

More so than the moment of death itself, many terminally ill adults are so fearful of the **process** *of dying that they don't want to think about it, much less speak of it. It may be that they have helped care for dying loved ones and now fear the weeks of decline, immobility, and dependency. There are many other things that cause fear of the death process, including fear of emotional or physical suffering leading up to death. Sparing the family from suffering during the final weeks is another motivation spoken of, but the loss of bodily control is most likely an overriding concern. The inability to walk or to maintain bladder/bowel continence is unthinkable to many and a flashpoint of fear so strong they want to bypass it. Some adults may only have known death that occurred in a hospital setting and have never observed or participated in the support and comfort of hospice care.*

People who are very uncomfortable about losing autonomy may wish to shorten the death process after receiving a terminal diagnosis. Doing so requires some planning and professional oversight. If this is something that appeals to you in your scenario, it is never too early to think about it. Therefore, the terminally ill should make and execute such a plan before becoming cognitively incapacitated in order for their choice to meet legal requirements. Should the time come that this becomes a consideration for you, it must be first discussed with your physician.

Other hospice patients, especially those sickened by multiple cancer treatments, may say they are simply tired of feeling ill for so long, of swallowing multiple pills, or of not feeling able to engage in chosen activities. Commonly, individuals describe growing "fed up" with living for so long in a way that they feel offers no quality of life. These individuals will often say they want a faster route to the end. The following methods can foreshorten the death process.

AID IN DYING

It should be noted that the remarks about aid in dying are not intended to represent the position of hospice or any medical entity, nor do the authors of this book necessarily endorse or condemn aid in dying. The general information and resources are provided for informational and planning purposes only.

Available now in a handful of states, a somewhat limited method to shorten the dying process is known by the legal name "aid in dying." It is also sometimes known by the inaccurate and misleading term "assisted suicide." This movement has received much national attention as individuals have sought to have choice in their death process. Aid in dying is intended as a compassionate option and is available as of this writing to eligible terminally ill patients in Oregon, California, Vermont, Washington, and Montana. As of 2017, Washington, DC and New York State are in the final stages of examining whether to also allow this remedy. Research also shows that one out of three qualified persons who obtain the medication do not utilize the option to take it. For more detailed understanding of this remedy, families in the states where this option is legal can visit www.DeathwithDignity.com, a non-profit organization website. This group will assist eligible individuals in locating resources to enable the terminally ill client to utilize the aid in dying within their state.

Aid in dying enables an eligible physician-qualified client to self-administer and ingest a lethal dose of prescribed medication after having completed a series of clearly defined steps to end one's life under specific laws within the states where it is permitted. A candidate for this option must have legal capacity (a sound state of mind) when requesting the dosage and must be able to self-administer the remedy. Research on patients who used aid in dying in Oregon as of 2007 indicates that complications do occur about 6 percent of the time, with regurgitation as the most common one. According to "Oregon Death with Dignity Act: 2015 Data Summary," the median time from ingestion to death is twenty-five minutes with a range up to forty-eight hours.

There are many philosophical, spiritual, and practical things to consider before settling on or acting on aid in dying. Hospice patients who choose aid in dying still receive hospice services, excluding assistance with ingestion of a life-taking drug. The patient must be able to self-administer the drugs.

I recommend considering carefully the reasons why an accelerated death is desired and what it would accomplish. For example, if avoiding pain and suffering is the primary motivation to choose aid in dying, hospice care is about relieving pain and calming patients during the natural death process.

VOLUNTARY STOPPING EATING AND DRINKING (VSED)

For those dying at home, another method to shorten the dying process that is compatible with hospice care is to voluntarily stop eating and drinking in advance of the active dying process. Loss of interest in food and drink is part of the natural death process, but choosing to fast to death is a legal choice that can be made in advance while an individual has mental capacity to do so. This option, available in all states, allows anyone with capacity to exercise their own legal medical decision to cease all intake of nourishment and fluids. Comfort medications are still administered. VSED usually results in a peaceful death within two weeks. It should be noted that state law may not allow skilled nursing facilities to support a patient in VSED.

This plan should be considered for mention in one's advanced health directives. Because this method is enacted when one is terminally ill, it can be problematic to enact if one has lost mental capacity or if one is residing in a facility where management is reluctant to allow a patient to die in this manner. Again, as suggested in the section on dementia, I recommend you include it along with a videotape of your wishes as another layer of security should this option be available in the future to you as a demented terminal patient.

To arrange VSED as a hospice patient, the person who is ill arranges to meet with the family and/or care team to attain understanding and agreement with this difficult decision. Of course, one must inform the patient's medical doctor, who should consult with hospice appropriately. If the patient is not already on hospice, they can request physician referral to hospice.

It is essential to have the consent of all caretakers and to know one's plan will be maintained throughout the process. This can be an unnerving idea for loved ones, so the discussion is likely to be emotionally charged with varied points of view. It is important to have agreement from the patient's spouse for support, and it is advisable to have a hospice team or team member present to assist in providing medical and technical explanation, as well as reassurance to family members. Among other things, the hospice team will remind the patient he/she can change their mind and revoke the plan during the first week. Once decided, caretakers are advised to offer food and fluids for the first forty-eight hours, to verify commitment of the sick person to the plan. For the remainder of the first week, no food will be offered unless the patient requests it. After the first week of not eating, it is unlikely they will be alert enough to make a request for food; by this point most patients will have progressed toward deeper slumber.

Once intake has stopped, thirst and hunger may persist, thirst more so. Ice chips may ease thirst for the first few days while the patient can still swallow. Multiple products are now available in the form of moisturizing gels, sprays, mouthwashes, and toothpastes to allay thirst very effectively when the patient cannot or will not intake fluids. After three to five days, hunger and thirst will gradually cease as one's body secretes natural hormones causing sleep and pain relief. Normally, comfort medications such as narcotics (pain) and anxiolytics (for restlessness) are offered. The person takes to bed and becomes quite sleepy within the first week. As days pass, lethargy increases until sleep overtakes consciousness. Death ensues quietly, usually before the end of the second week.

Voluntary stopping of eating and drinking (a legal term) mimics the natural dying process when people unconsciously lose interest in nourishment. It also allows time to say goodbyes to loved ones and time to examine one's life in preparation for its end. The non-profit California educational group website www.CaringAdvocates.org has detailed information, including videos, on this subject.

FUNERAL PLANNING

We strongly advocate for being open about death and for individuals to "design" various aspects of their end of life, so it also makes good sense to pre-plan one's funeral. Some adults would argue this is just too disagreeable a topic, yet many report achieving peace of mind once their death planning is complete.

There are many options to be identified in planning your funeral and the interment of your body or ashes. Each state regulates the practices of body disposal so there may be differences in the choices available in your state. I have briefly described most of the choices one will face below, but keep in mind that any questions you have can be answered by a call to your local funeral director.

To begin, you should think about how you want your remains handled. The main choices currently are whole-body burial, body disintegration through either cremation or chemical dissolution, or body donation. Body freezing, or cryonics, is a minor, rarely used option with different goals that require a different planning method.

Embalming remains the most common practice for whole-body burials, but some states allow the "greener" option of burial without chemical preservation. In the practice of the latter, one might also choose an eco-friendly or biodegradable casket in lieu of the traditional metal or wood casket. It should be noted there are differences between eco-friendly and green burials as defined by the funeral industry. One should be clear about the differences before choosing. Not all funeral businesses offer green preservation and burials or eco-friendly choices.

If a traditional cemetery is the choice, once that location is identified, the casket can be interred in the ground, a crypt, or a mausoleum. In a green cemetery, the casket is placed into the ground without a headstone with the goal of returning the body and materials to the environment in an organically healthy way. Estate or family plots also exist on private land, where special permits allow.

Alternatives to whole-body burial include cremation or alkaline hydrolysis, either of which reduces the remains to a box of ash. Ashes can be placed into a vessel and then buried in the ground or placed into a wall at a cemetery. Some choose to distribute the ashes freely into a body of water, the air, or by other means. Others choose to place the vessel in the home in perpetuity. Before deciding to scatter ashes, it is important to understand state regulations. Doing so is outlawed in many areas. A local funeral home may be able to provide information regarding these regulations.

Whole-body donations for research and education can be an important means for supporting medical education and research while potentially minimizing the costs of body disposition. Some medical schools or organizations require pre-registration, others do not. It is important to thoroughly investigate how an organization will use the donation before making your choice. It is up to the organization to use the body as they require, so the person planning end of life should be comfortable with that goal. Pre-registering allows one to confirm the organization goals are a match for yours. Once notified, the organization will send paperwork for you to complete and return. <u>Enrollment does not guarantee acceptance of the body donation at time of death.</u> Some conditions and infectious diseases will be screened out. Extreme obesity or low body weight may also make the donation unsuitable.

Completely separate and distinct from whole-body donations, specific organ donation is normally generated within a hospital setting where a sudden death has occurred. If one dies in a slow process of natural decline at home, organ donation is not an option as the goal is to use a healthy organ to extend life for another person. That said, we can't predict how death will come, so I would encourage you to plan for organ donation in the event your death comes suddenly. Organ donation is worthy of our consideration and one donor can save multiple lives.

Active military personnel and honorably discharged veterans are eligible for military honors at their funerals and for burial in a military cemetery, so long as they have completed one term enlisted or in the Selected Reserves. These services must be requested by the funeral director and include the American Flag folding ceremony and the playing of "Taps," either live or recorded.

Pre-paid funeral plans are a good way to help loved ones when you are gone. Typically, funeral homes belong to an association that assures the services can be provided even if the contracted individual has relocated to another part of the country. Again, be sure loved ones can find the paperwork for your pre-paid arrangements.

CHAPTER SUMMARY

- Most people you know would say they prefer a sudden death or to die in their sleep. A quiet, peaceful death or dying in one's sleep is what hospice facilitates.
- One can and should plan for death as though it might happen tomorrow, natural or otherwise.
- Planning and making known one's wishes to a spouse or legal agent makes their job easier.
- Despite the bad news of a terminal diagnosis, immediate attention to financial planning, addressing legal matters, and planning for one's burial can provide tremendous comfort to the terminal patient and the family.
- Natural death is an active, productive time of one's life during which one can find resolution and peace.
- Putting end-of-life decisions in a written legal format protects the decisions and those who carry them out from interference. Even more important, it prevents the terminal individual from being subjected to unpleasant life-extending measures.
- Since most people die a natural death following a slow health decline, it is wise to also look ahead and make plans for having help when one becomes infirm.
- Dementia will affect nearly half of the senior population. In many cases, one's body can be kept alive despite apparent inability to participate in or enjoy life. It is recommended

that planning include how much life-support be given once a patient cannot self-feed, communicate, or interact.

- Even if patients request it, doctors are not required to deliver treatment that delivers no benefit, so it is important to have compassionate medical providers who will realistically discuss ending aggressive treatment.

- Creative plans for helping seniors on limited incomes pay for their lifestyle and late-life care needs should be carefully considered. Financial advice from a disinterested third party is recommended. Consideration of options like a reverse mortgage should not be taken lightly—it's not the best choice for everyone. Aging in place (in one's own home) sounds good, but is not always the best environment as one's needs change and require accommodation.

- For adults with no family members or trusted friends to assist them in late life, having the care they need can be difficult to find and maintain. It is challenging and expensive to hire caregivers and requires the involvement of someone who can interview and coordinate hiring or selection of an agency or a professional care coordinator.

- There are options for shortening the dying process. Those decisions need to be made while the individual is of sound mind and handled in accordance with the laws of the state. Hospice is designed to alleviate the pain and suffering many people often fear so that natural death can complete its course.

Resources

AARP
www.aarp.org/home-family/caregiving

Council on Aging
www.coaoc.org/resources/resources-for-caregivers.aspx

www.caregiving.com
www.Benefitscheckup.org
www.Eldercare.gov
www.Benefits.gov
www.FamilyCareNavigator.org

National Hospice and Palliative Care Organization (NHPCO)
www/nhpco.org

National Healthcare Decisions Day
www.nhdd.org

Coalition for Compassionate Care of California
www.coalitionccc.org
www.agingwithdignity.org
www.caringadvocates.org

Modern Death

How Medicine Changed the End of Life, Haider Warraich, MD.
Published in 2017, this book offers an updated view of
end of life issues from a cardiologist's viewpoint.

Funeral information

www.funeralplanning101.com
www.funeralinspirations.co.uk
www.newoldage.blogs.nytimes.com/2012/02/14/
alternatives-to-the-traditional-funeral/
www.greenburialcouncil.org/

For more information on military cemeteries and funerals, go to www.
military.com or call 1-800-827-1000. Here one can learn eligibility factors
for honors and financial funeral stipends for eligible active duty veterans.

Chapter Three

THE DRAGON YEAR

SOMETHING IS WRONG

"Honey."

His voice sounded strange as his endearment for me was drawn out in that tone of disbelief tinged with alarm.

"Paula! Come in here! I need you to see this."

I had just set Jim's breakfast on the table and was preparing a lunch for him to take to his part-time security job. Now I dropped everything and took a second to compose myself, disturbed by the sound of his voice. I'd never heard this tone from Jim before. Did he actually sound scared?

The hallway to the master bedroom was dark and I couldn't imagine what I would see upon entering the room. I did know that Jim would not have called me to the room if there was something bad that could happen to me. Then I saw what I saw and knew something bad had happened to both of us.

* * *

For a moment I stood transfixed, memories of the recent summer (2011) flooding back to me. Unlike the husbands of many of my friends, Jim was a rare man in that he would always go to the doctor when health issues arose. Most of my friends were chronically frustrated by husbands who would delay seeing the doctor even if they were in pain. Jim seemed to prefer to get to the doctor and have matters cleared up quickly. I was grateful for that but a few months back, I had to nudge him quite insistently to get him to see the doctor.

Up until this time, Jim seemed healthy and his only complaint was a mild frustration that his waistline seemed to be expanding despite his efforts to maintain it. Being overweight myself, I assumed his body was succumbing to gravity and sixty-eight years of life. We knew my problem was about diet and exercise but Jim had always been able to easily maintain or make minor corrections to his weight. Jim hated having to purchase pants with relaxed waistbands or moving up a waist size, which he had done twice in the past year or so. At that point in time, I did not recognize his increased girth as anything more than an age and fitness issue.

But then, Jim began to have night sweats. These were not like my hot flashes that induced perspiration, but something whose origins were deep within him. Each time he was left drenched and the bed covers required immediate removal and washing. He felt well the rest of the time, maintaining his routine of part-time work, weekly poker with his friends, yard work, and golfing a couple times each week. To him, a little sweat seemed harmless. To me, in this volume, it was a reminder of the early signs of my father's non-Hodgkins lymphoma. When Jim's night sweats began to happen a couple times each week, I insisted we see our family physician, Dr. Robert Rutherford, at our local Alexander Valley Healthcare facility.

It was a blessing to us at this time that our rural healthcare facility had scored a physician whose education and medical pedigrees included the University of Washington, Stanford, Johns Hopkins and Harvard. He served in the Peace Corps and was a founder of the Haight Ashbury Clinic in San Francisco. Having more recently served as an emergency room physician, Dr. Rutherford was adept at being presented with problems and drilling quickly through symptoms and test results to determine next steps.

I didn't want to alarm Jim with my concerns by mentioning my father, but I felt this night sweat symptom was definitely a bad sign. Jim had a condition his previous doctor had referred to as "chronic leukemia" that had not given him any problems during our marriage. Leukemia was something Dr. Rutherford wanted to look into. He did blood draws and took an updated and in-depth history. After listening to Jim give him what I thought was incomplete information, I finally could not help but speak out and suggest another potential cause—the one my father had died from in 2001. After all, both Jim and my father spent lots of time on the golf course and my research suggested some medical experts thought there could be a connection between golf course maintenance chemicals and certain blood cancers. By sharing that, I was hoping to help eliminate a few tangents and arrive more quickly at an actual diagnosis, which I was sure would be treatable. Dr. Rutherford signaled that he heard me but his process was underway and he proceeded with the examination without responding to me verbally. When the appointment was over, we left to await a call to come back and discuss results of the blood tests.

Upon return to the health care center, we learned the tests were inconclusive. Jim had experienced no more episodes of night sweats for a couple weeks, but I wanted to look further into what had seemed to me to be abnormal and extreme. Jim was finished. He wanted to get back to his fishing and his other retirement activities. It was as though he thought the sweats had been a mere blip while I saw them as something more ominous. He was in charge and he angrily shut me down in front of the doctor when I attempted to argue for more investigation. The doctor saw compromise was needed and suggested it would be a good idea to check back in a month or two to retest, sooner if symptoms returned or new ones arose. It had not occurred to either of us that summer to mention to the doctor Jim's gradually expanding waistline. I wonder now if we had done so whether the doctor might have ordered a scan that would have revealed the problem sooner.

Those months passed and Jim still did not wish to pursue investigation of the now absent symptoms. The night sweats were concerning to me and I was a little angry he would not take them seriously. However, I decided it was Jim's decision and I hoped it was for the best. He enjoyed that summer so, looking back, perhaps it was for the best.

* * *

I was not prepared for what I saw when I entered the bedroom.

"I can't fit into my pants; not even close," he said with a mix of disbelief and panic. "I can barely button my shirt. What is going on?"

There stood my husband, tall, hair still damp from the shower, eyes big and full of questions. "How am I going to work today if I can't dress myself?"

My six-foot-plus husband weighed about 220 pounds. There he stood before me with a distended stomach that mimicked a late stage pregnancy—twins. I stared and blinked, unable to understand what I was seeing. He had gone to bed before me the previous night without making complaint. He had risen before me to shower and I suppose I hadn't really looked at his body until then. Jim was a man of routines and responsibilities. I knew it would take some convincing but he had to see a doctor immediately. I spoke in a voice that I hoped would be commanding enough to avoid argument.

"Simple. You are calling your supervisor and telling him you have to see a doctor. This," I said, pointing to his middle, "is not normal. You aren't going anywhere until we find out what your doctor says. I'll call for an appointment."

My eyes were filling with tears as I turned away and went to the kitchen to once again call Alexander Valley Healthcare. It was December 9, 2011, a Friday. Jim called to explain to his supervisor at the security job that he would not be in that day. I was determined nothing would get in the way of us seeing a doctor before the weekend. Fortunately, Dr. Rutherford was working that day, and he fit us in early that afternoon.

As he examined Jim, I watched closely. It was not so much the examination but the doctor's eyes that I watched. And there I saw it for the first time. I don't know if it was fear or sadness, but bad news was smoldering in his eyes. When he spoke, I felt his words were more measured and his tone of voice especially modulated to be gentle and calming. I tried to hold my own demeanor in check for Jim's sake. The unknown was scary enough. I could not overreact.

After telling us several diseases he had ruled out, Dr. Rutherford wanted Jim to be seen by a gastroenterologist right away. The calendar was closing in on the holidays and doctors were overwhelmed with year-end visits so patients could make the most of already paid deductibles. Dr. Rutherford suggested that we see a specialist in Ukiah rather than going to Santa Rosa, where medical facilities would likely be booked in full. The medical centers were equal distances in opposite directions but he believed Jim would be seen sooner in Ukiah. We were sent home to await a call with the assurance that Dr. Rutherford would help guide us to the places where answers would be found as quickly as possible.

Much sooner than we expected, we received word Jim had an appointment at the end of the day with a Ukiah gastroenterologist. The specialist had stayed beyond his normal workday schedule to see us. In the past, whenever Jim had been referred by a family doctor for further treatment, the next step was to resolve a known matter, and it had always proved sufficient, so Jim remained fairly calm given that history. Usually an optimist, I could not help feeling alarmed—doctors typically make last-minute scheduling exceptions when the need is greatest. I said nothing to Jim about that. I was doing my best to be positive, upbeat, and to not transfer my concerns to him. Instead, we talked about how nice it would be to get some answers quickly.

It was dark and cold at 7:00 p.m. when we emerged bewildered from the second examination of the day. The doctor could not be specific other than to say the exam had not provided answers that would have indicated a relatively easy fix. He had already forwarded information to Dr. Rutherford's office, and we would hear from Dr. Rutherford on Monday as to next steps.

"I'm so sorry. Good luck," were his parting words.

What could that mean?

It was just the first time we would hear "I'm so sorry" from a medical professional. The most cheerful thought I could offer on the way home was that at least we did not have to wait over the weekend for Jim to get the process started in solving his mystery. He was still not showing signs of alarm other than at his obvious physical change. I don't know if he was still processing the new information and still unclear that his situation was likely very serious. Perhaps he was alarmed and didn't want to upset me. We talked around the matter. What should he say to his supervisor? He wondered whether there would be more tests that would prevent him from working for a week or two. I expected there would be but felt it was Dr. Rutherford's job to break that news. No need to worry Jim through the weekend.

Too many unknowns loomed, so we tried to be "normal." I shopped for Jim's favorite foods and he attempted to relish my efforts, but meal times were quieter than usual. He left the house to be outdoors down by the river. I worried about him being down there alone in the cold, but I knew he needed privacy and time to think. He took our beloved poodle BD with him (for comfort, I suspected). We could have used two BDs. That evening I made a weak excuse for going out and ran to my friend Antonella's house to cry at her kitchen table so I could come home and hold my head high for Jim. It was to be the first of many tearful sessions with her.

UNRAVELING THE MYSTERY

Following discussion with Dr. Rutherford about the gastroenterology report, he began arranging the next step in the medical discovery process. Jim did not complain much of discomfort, but he was continually challenged to find clothes that were comfortable. He began wearing his pants below his belly and loose-fitting, untucked shirts. At his weekly poker game with his friends, he shared this new experience. The guys expressed to him a friendly interest in his comfort but it was many months later, after we knew the truth, that they told me how Jim's sharing of this first sudden physical change had worried them.

The word "cancer" had already crept into our conversations as soon as Jim and I learned we would see an oncologist for the next step in his diagnosis. However, hearing that word *from* an oncologist took us from imagining a scary scenario to beginning to live it.

In the week following his visit to the gastroenterologist, Jim was referred to an oncologist at Ukiah Valley Medical Center to begin ruling out various diagnoses. Dr. Russell Hardy took a genuine interest in his patients. He came to know *who* they were as much as *how* they were. Unlike some physicians I'd heard about, Dr. Hardy and his staff never seemed to lose sight of the fact that new patients were terrified to see him. Jim was sent for a battery of blood tests, to radiology, and to have a small amount of the fluid that swelled his mid-section examined. Dr. Hardy was very good at giving information in measured, digestible doses. When we pressed for more information, he was careful about committing to a diagnosis of which he could not be 100 percent sure. He mentioned mesothelioma at one point, but would only share what he knew in a way the patient could process, and was honest in his delivery of the hard facts.

It was now time for a surgical exploration and biopsy. Dr. Hardy explained that the fluid accumulating around Jim's waistline was his body's response to the growth of cancer. Jim was now complaining regularly about discomfort in his distended midsection. When asked about removing all of it to make Jim more comfortable, the doctor explained they had to be careful not to create further problems by disturbing diseased tissue and damaging organs. Hardy was seeking confirmation as to the type of cancer, but the tests and examinations had so far only revealed Jim was in late stages.

I wanted to blurt out a lot of questions but could not talk through my tears. I had seen friends endure cancer treatment and could not bear the thought of my wonderful husband having to suffer. Jim sat in stunned silence. I was unaware he did not fully understand that the term "stage 4" meant his disease had progressed very far, to a point that is most often incurable.

NOT-SO-MERRY CHRISTMAS

On December 22 we returned to Dr. Russell's office to learn what we could from the additional tests he had done. This would be an important visit because it was all we would have to get us through the end-of-year holidays. Again, the news was not good, but we had come to expect more bad news each visit until the final diagnosis. Following the explanation that Dr. Hardy was still attempting to confirm the type of cancer to determine best treatment options, he was able to answer some of Jim's questions. Jim hung his head when told he would not be cured. Our next step would be a visit with a surgeon to learn the extent of the disease and see what options might be most advisable. That was scheduled for after the year-end holidays.

When he recovered from the weight of that information sufficiently, Jim asked, "So how long do I have to live?"

Dr. Hardy explained that lifespan is difficult for any doctor to predict, but that he thought if Jim lived until next Christmas (2012), that he "would have lived a good, long time" with the disease. He added that it was fully possible Jim could live up to two years, depending on the options available once diagnosis was completed and Jim's treatment choices. Again, Jim hung his head to absorb this because we all wanted him to live more than two years. Dr. Hardy took this moment to explain to Jim that it would be wise to make his end-of-life plans in the upcoming weeks because once the diagnosis was finalized, it was likely he would begin receiving chemotherapy and his days would be filled with medical appointments and possibly unwelcome side effects.

We were hurtling toward Christmas with little cheer in our hearts.

"I don't want my girls or anyone in the family to know anything until after Christmas. I mean that," Jim insisted.

I nodded agreement. It was Jim's call and I was there to support him. Besides, we were enduring the pain of having his life-shortening health condition revealed to us in excruciatingly small pieces. Why put his family through that? Better to give them the full story so they could deal with the initial pain one time. Moreover, it was Jim's life and he had to be in charge of those decisions and choices

Jim didn't even need to say it; I knew it was time to practice my holiday smile in front of the mirror and find a way to cover the darkening circles under my eyes, the result of restless nights. We would have a "normal" holiday with the family and they would never know that our lives had been turned upside-down. On Christmas Day, each time I hit a bump in the road while driving to the family holiday gathering at his daughter Roberta's house, Jim would be so miserable he would shout at me. I burst into tears when he castigated me for hitting a manhole cover as though I was trying to make him feel uncomfortable. I managed to get my emotions in check before we went into Roberta's house.

Jim wore an untucked plaid wool shirt that fairly well minimized the appearance of his bulging middle. Nobody even seemed to notice when they hugged him. Jim was amazingly strong throughout the day, teasing his grandchildren and visiting individually with his daughters and sons-in-law while I admired his capacity to protect this day for his family. At one point I retreated to the powder room to get through a teary moment. Jim gave me a knowing look when I emerged, but none of the others seemed to notice the red-rimmed eyes behind my eyeglasses. I began to focus on my acting skills because Jim deserved an Oscar-worthy performance from me, and we apparently both did a pretty good job.

We kept our brave faces on even at home in an attempt to enjoy our quiet holiday by the fireplace with the dogs. Finally, in the week between Christmas and New Year's Day, Jim decided to call his daughters to the house. Renee and Roberta both knew something urgent was happening and seemed afraid when they arrived, perhaps because their father insisted they find a way to arrange their day and come at the same time. That was unusual.

I can't imagine what other bad news they might have imagined, because they seemed stunned to learn the subject was a matter of health and mortality. Jim plainly outlined what he knew and admitted many questions remained unanswered. Renee wept quietly into her hands and asked questions about how long he had known. Roberta, the youngest who shared a January 12 birthday with her father, wailed and raced to be sick in the bathroom.

Once somewhat composed, my step-daughters' reactions were typical based on what I've come to understand about the variety of human responses to news of impending death. The eldest asked questions and volunteered her support, asking us to keep her informed of her father's status and what she could do to help. The younger, wanting so badly to believe her father could not possibly be in mortal danger, declared she would take charge of her father's care and solve the problem. Once our limited cache of answers was exhausted, Jim promised we would keep them informed. He also reined in his youngest with a promise to hear her suggestions but firmly relieved her of any perceived responsibility for his healthcare decisions. He would make the decisions and her step-mom would be in charge of carrying them out.

For the next week or so, Jim chose not to be around our friends. In some way, it seemed having acknowledged his situation to his children made it more real to him and he needed to take that in. For a time, he did not want to be with our usual Saturday night dinner friends, and tended to prefer his poker and golf buddies because they could be together supporting one another without discussing the elephant in the room. He telephoned his uncle and aunt in Oregon, as well as other special people, to tell them what was happening. He longed to go back to work to take his mind off his situation and because he felt he was letting his supervisor down. Jim's mid-section was making him miserable, so we were both anxious to have the surgical procedure that would pave the way for his first paracentesis appointment to drain the ascites fluid buildup in his abdomen.

OTHER-WORLDLY GUIDANCE

Our next step in January 2012 was a visit with Dr. Ziad Hanna, who would surgically explore the extent of the disease and obtain a biopsy. Dr. Hanna had an incredibly kind demeanor and we both felt immediately confident Jim would receive excellent care from him.

When we returned to see Dr. Hanna in his office after the surgery, I remember his kind face and dark, sympathetic eyes. He confirmed that Jim had stage 4 cancer, meaning it had metastasized, or spread far from the original site. He mentioned mesothelioma, the second time we heard that might be a possibility, but it remained unconfirmed. I wasn't clear at the time why the diagnosis was so difficult but I, like others, believed mesothelioma to be a lung disease. If that was so, why were they looking in the peritoneal sac where Jim's other organs resided? Why was his stomach so distended? It was that point in the process when each piece of new information led to more questions and the answers most often led to more bad news.

Following his medical explanations, Dr. Hanna quietly spoke to us as a friend, gently and firmly suggesting we listen carefully to what he had to say. He urged us to summon strength from our higher power, though I don't recall those specific words. He then shared a piece of advice that became pivotal in Jim's life and mine. The quotes that follow are not exact, but convey the meaning of what we were told.

"There will be people out there who will insist you try this or that treatment and that you have more surgery," he said. "But I want you to always think first of quality of life. This is important: before you make any decision about treatment, ask yourself how it will affect your quality of life for the time remaining."

What happened next I can only describe as divine. I once wrote a letter to Dr. Hanna thanking him for his kindness and medical expertise in my husband's case, but I never told him this. He rose from behind his desk and came to me. I was distraught beyond anything I had ever experienced—the pain was so great I thought it might consume me. I cannot say if the doctor approached me because I was to be Jim's caregiver or because he related to my pain as a spouse. Perhaps he had encountered spouses like my mother who could not hear of her husband's terminal condition. I would have expected him to comfort Jim, but there he was next to me.

As much as I tried to stop crying, I could only stifle the noises in my throat—the tears were uncontrollable. I wanted to wail out loud and bury my face in his shoulder. I knew now I was about to experience the biggest loss in my life since my father had died in 2001.

Strangely, instead of patting Jim's shoulder as I would have thought, Dr. Hanna placed his hand on the crown of my head. A presence filled me up that took my breath away.

"You have a very difficult time ahead. It will be a painful journey but there is also joy." I felt the full force of my father's presence speaking to me through Dr. Hanna as he repeated his advice about focusing on quality of life. It is the only time my father has come to me since his death. A quiet man, my father saved words for the greatest effect. The rest of the words were lost in the emotion and revelation of the moment. I was aware Jim was in the room, but have no idea what he experienced as I took in this emotional and spiritual phenomenon. The communication was so unusual I have since considered whether Dr. Hanna had psychic abilities or was simply a conduit that enabled my father to reach me with this powerful message so I would never forget it.

Despite my anguish in that formidable moment, I began to feel empowered to partner my husband through what I now understood would be an ordeal. As we said our goodbyes, Dr. Hanna saw us to the side door for privacy and told us we would see Dr. Hardy the next week for more information and to start making a plan. "Think quality of life," he said one more time. He then generously told us we could call him and make an appointment any time we needed to discuss our situation.

Jim and I sat silently in the car for a few minutes before I started the engine. It was a sunny, cold, dry January day during Northern California's drought, but the sun warmed the car. The meeting was so emotionally charged, I needed to calm myself before driving. I couldn't imagine what was taking place in Jim's thoughts, but he was also silenced by what he had just been through. I was trying to pull myself together to begin "being there" for him, so I had no idea if he was frightened or in denial or if he, too, had experienced something as unusual as my father's presence was to me.

I finally started the car and we began the drive home in silence. As I pulled away from the medical center parking lot I was still scared and upset, but the extraordinary sensation of my father's touch remained with me. I knew my soul would be transformed by the upcoming journey Jim and I would share. My father lived on the other side of the country, so I had not been available to care for him, though I had visited when I could. I would now have that important role of caregiver for my husband and I would do whatever it took make sure his suffering was minimized.

I think it was Jim who turned on the radio to help fill the silence. What occurred next seemed to be directed to and belong exclusively to Jim. A familiar and popular country song of the day began. We both listened carefully for the first time to the words of Tim McGraw's "Live Like You Were Dying." The timing of that message struck both of us as meaningful and mysterious, though it probably was played numerous times every day.

"Well. I guess that's clear. Strange that song played now, right?"

I agreed that we both were hearing the same message and that it was hard to hear, but that it sounded like good advice. Jim seemed very calm at this moment, considering his situation.

BEING MY BEST FOR JIM

Needless to say, the January 12 joint birthday we always celebrated with Roberta's family for her and her father was not the usual jovial event in 2012. We tried, but emotions and questions crept into the party. It could not be helped because the idea of Jim's disease took up so much real estate in all our brains. This was especially so because that same week, the firm diagnosis came in and the doctors were no longer tentative in their conversation with us. Jim's disease was now confirmed as stage 4 peritoneal mesothelioma and most definitely terminal. He would not likely live longer than a couple years and it was now time to make major care decisions. That night we explained to his family several times the difference between peritoneal mesothelioma and the more common occurrence of the disease in the lung. Beyond that, we knew nothing. On the positive side, Jim could now begin to have the fluid drained from his abdomen to alleviate some discomfort.

Since that last visit with Dr. Hardy, all hope had abandoned me like air rapidly escaping from an untied balloon. I was deflated, depleted, and despairing. I didn't sleep more than a few hours that entire week. We had hired landscapers to install a water-saving makeover in our side yard, but when they came to the door one morning to start work, I was completely out of control and unable to communicate.

It was as though I had split into two beings—one who was unable to control her mouth and thoughts, and another that knew something was wrong but could only watch with embarrassment. My arms waved wildly as I talked and I could not string together a sentence. I could see the workers looking at one another and understood why they were confused. Appalled and embarrassed, I could only retreat behind the front door, wondering who I had become.

I called Dr. Rutherford, also my physician, and was surprised that he took me right away. Alone in the examining room with him, I found myself behaving in the same inexplicable way as I tried to explain to him that I knew I needed help. I cried in grief and frustration. His look was one of understanding. He promised to help me and to be available to me as I helped my husband through his journey. The first building block of my care plan was a sleep prescription. Yes, it could be habit-forming for some people, but he advised that I would be of no help to Jim and my own health would decline if I did not sleep. I would come see him every thirty days to check in before getting another prescription.

As soon as I began taking the medication, I was able to once again enjoy sweet sleep. However, after a few days, I noticed I was groggy most of the morning. With a call to Dr. Rutherford, the dosage was adjusted and I was once again well rested and feeling energized after a night's sleep. I apologized to my husband and to the landscape crew for my crazy behavior, which was beyond embarrassing to me. But now I felt more clear-headed than any time during our first part on this journey. Well rested, I could get through each day and be available to my husband in any way he required. I knew that being a caregiver required me to take good care of myself. I had been around caregivers and had helped others in our family enough to fully understand the importance of self-care.

We went through some serious ups and downs in the early part of 2012. Initially it seemed each medical visit revealed something new and disturbing. We then entered a phase during which Jim explored options as to treatment, including clinical trials and new surgical procedures that at first seemed hopeful, but often left us low again when it was determined Jim was not a candidate.

As much as Jim struggled with all of this, I too struggled to comfort him while grieving the growing reality of our situation. Once we entered this phase, Dr. Rutherford recommended I also take an anti-depressant. For those of you who avoid taking medicine at all costs, I can only offer my experience that these two medications, a sleep aid and an anti-depressant, made me alert and better in control of my emotions for the duration of Jim's experience than otherwise would have been the case. For me, that was important, and I feel it made a big difference for Jim that he did not have to watch me suffer when he needed my attention. This was all about Jim and I needed to give him my best.

JIM PLANS FOR HIS FAMILY

It was Jim's nature to take care of his family. One wish he expressed was to have a portrait of himself done for me. It was a lovely idea and he decided he would have our pets, BD the black poodle and the newly acquired Chihuahua Lily-Lou, included in the photo. I would take photos and we would send them to my artist friend, Chris Dec, for her artistic interpretation. We laughed each time we tried to put the dogs in the photo because they insisted on kissing one another and would not look at the camera. I finally had to settle for photographing Jim and each dog separately. The individual photographs were surprisingly good. Jim still looked so healthy and happy. He wore a favorite hat I had given him some years before and a manly flannel shirt Roberta had given him. A few weeks later we had a beautiful portrait of Jim with the dogs in an outdoor setting. It hangs in the den and makes me smile whenever I look at it. We had smaller versions made for Roberta and Renee.

Jim's investments were already in the hands of a bright young investor with our bank, but Jim was following advice from the doctor to look into his end-of-life planning. He had grown very fond of Daniel Brown, having years before been stung by an investment firm that took advantage of his modest holdings and saw him as an easy tap for fees. Daniel listened to Jim's goals and they talked about strategy together. Daniel responded in a very personal way to Jim's health dilemma and began to suggest new strategies. Over time, Daniel moved to another bank and ultimately formed his own firm. Jim decided to stay with him and shared with me that he wanted me to stay with Daniel in the future. Jim was a good judge of people.

Even as plans were being made to set up his chemotherapy, Jim decided he could no longer put off what we had talked about but never quite gotten around to: establishing trusts. We long ago had agreed that I would make sure his daughters received what he wanted them to have, but we needed to formalize everything. We began meeting with a recommended estate and trusts attorney. Janne O'Neil was patient and thorough. Over the course of a month or two, we worked out the legal arrangements for handling Jim's estate and mine, as well as signing advanced health care directives. As my husband was in the throes of confronting his end of life, this was a painful process at times. Still, he was determined to see it through and felt a tremendous sense of relief and pride when it was completed.

Also very helpful, a friend and neighbor, Cherie, referred us to a law firm that specialized in mesothelioma lawsuits and offered lots of information from her experience working in a law firm. Jeffrey Kaiser of Kaiser Gornick, LLP made the two-plus-hour drive to our home from San Francisco the day after I called him. He was very helpful and thorough in researching Jim's asbestos exposure, which could only have come from his service in the Navy. While researching the suppliers and contractors responsible for selling asbestos products used on the ships Jim served on, Kaiser also pulled in a renowned pathologist, Dr. Russell Salyer, to study Jim's case and write up an in-depth report for the Veteran's Administration using the records generated by Jim's doctors. Both gentlemen had done pro bono work for veterans suffering from mesothelioma as a result of their military service. Despite horror stories about veterans whose genuine needs remain unaddressed as their applications for Veteran's Administration benefits languish in the system, Jeffrey Kaiser's well-supported letter to the agency brought about a decision in Jim's favor within two weeks as the independent expert pathology report made the case undeniably clear. We were stunned and felt gratitude to both our attorney and the pathologist for their generosity and to the VA for their rapid response.

Jim had always been proud of his service in the US Navy. The VA support made him feel appreciated, despite the unfortunate health outcome. He was grateful to have our modest assets protected for his family. Later, when his changing situation required that we update records and make new applications for VA benefits on our own, we did encounter some challenges, but overall we felt blessed to have this boost to our modest financial situation. It gave Jim a greater sense of peace.

TREATMENT

After fully examining and exploring the extent of his cancer, Jim finally had the ascites fluid tapped from his belly area. Dr. Laura Ann Winkle, who headed the team performing that procedure, was very caring, as was the rest of the radiology staff working with her at UVMC. Jim felt immediate relief following the procedure, known as paracentesis. Despite the challenges ahead and upcoming chemotherapy, being more comfortable seemed to improve Jim's outlook for the time.

By February, Dr. Hardy had settled on the initial chemotherapy treatment that he felt was best. I will not address specifics of treatment and medications used because I don't want readers to interpret that I am advocating for any specific treatment. Those decisions can only be made between a patient and physician based on the patient's specific needs and treatment goals. After reviewing the options and talking with Jim about the goals of his treatment, I will simply say the doctor chose a "cocktail" and treatment plan intended to slow or temporarily halt progression of the disease, ideally with nominal side effects. There was some marginal possibility the treatment could achieve remission, but that could not be known until sometime into the treatment process. Dr. Hardy explained that he would make additional recommendations or adjustments after each round of treatments based on Jim's response. Palliative care was available, if that was of interest, but Jim seemed mostly comfortable as treatment proceeded. Perhaps because we did not fully understand what it could do for Jim, it did not occur to us to inquire about it further. Quite honestly, I assumed the critical time for pain management would be linked to hospice down the road when Jim was sicker. That is not always the case.

So the routine began. We scheduled blood draws, draining of ascites fluid, and chemo sessions in Ukiah so that most often two of the three were accomplished the same day. The drive to Ukiah through the rolling hills of southern Mendocino County was beautiful, especially in the spring, and it had a calming effect on both of us. In preparation for days when there would be a long wait between appointments, Jim would bring his fishing rod and we would go to Lake Mendocino after his blood draw until it was time to go for his chemo or paracentesis appointment. Jim made friends with staff in each office of the medical center that handled his case, as well as a few of the chemo patients who were able to put up with his silly sense of humor. He was determined that chemo treatments and doctor visits would not be a dreary part of his day. Sometimes we stopped for lunch. Even on the hard days, we looked forward to the beautiful ride home through the Northern California countryside. By late spring, the ride home sometimes included a stop at a popular roadside strawberry farm. We made the trips as pleasant as possible and took advantage of having quiet time together.

A METAPHOR FOR STRENGTH AND WISDOM

2012 was the Year of the Dragon, celebrated in the most colorful and spectacular way in San Francisco's Chinatown. I selected the powerful aspects of my birth sign as a personal theme and suitable metaphor for what that year would surely bring to my life. The dragon was, after all, the only mythical creature in the Chinese zodiac. Even the phoenix did not make the grade. As I saw it, I would need to harness the powers of the Universe that reside within all of us to do a good job for Jim and to survive our shared journey. I had long wanted to attend the Chinese New Year celebration. Several of my closest girlfriends supported my goal to attend the parade as a way to symbolically stoke my inner strength in order to support Jim. They immediately signed up for the quest.

It must be said at this time that my friends were the glue that held me together from the time Jim became ill to this day. No matter what I need, I can call on them. Paulette and Chris were more than happy to go with me to San Francisco to see the parade. Paulette invited another friend to join us and we headed south talking about the wonderful lunch of authentic Chinese food we would enjoy in Chinatown to start our adventure.

The early February parade day started beautifully. First, a good parking place. Then, colorful sights as families strolled the parade route soaking up the cultural experience. It started so nicely, but it turned out we all needed dragon strength to survive that event. The sights revved up our appetites, but the Chinese meal we had was weird and inedible. I had never before seen a Chinese menu that included borscht and some sort of overcooked pork chops with a gelatinous pink sauce on them. The marginal menu pictures were not nearly as unappetizing as the actual meals when they arrived at the table. This, despite thinking our plan to identify a good restaurant was foolproof—we asked an official-looking individual at the Chinese Chamber of Commerce office. There is more to the story, but suffice it to say we left hungry, our plates barely touched.

Next, we decided to have a celebratory drink at a nearby bar before the parade. Even my drink was terrible: a Cosmopolitan so tart it gave me an unquenchable thirst. I was still hungry but after everyone finished their drinks, we needed to hurry to find our place on the sidelines to watch the parade. I had dragged my friends along for my benefit, so I allowed them to choose the spot. Their "chooser" was off on that day because we wound up in a terrible place where the view was cut off by the reviewing stand until parade elements were immediately in front of us. The split-second appearances of parade entries gave us no time to get good pictures of the amazing sights.

As daylight grew dim, young men who enjoyed injecting a little fright into the festivities began throwing firecrackers at our feet. As more time passed, some drunken members of the crowd began pushing us into the crowd barriers. One small elderly woman fell and had to be helped up. We began to panic. When a police officer finally moved some spectators along, creating a break in the sea of bodies, my friends and I joined hands and took off to a side street. We discovered a nice café around the corner, just feet away from the parade route. Apple fritters and tea never tasted so good.

From our café table, we could clearly see the parade and felt much safer than we had on the street. Now completely dark outside, the costumes of the dancing Chinese zodiac creatures were spectacularly lit. We finally stepped outside to a slightly elevated and uncrowded side street that allowed us to get a few snapshots at the final turnaround of the parade route. There was a breathtaking view of the magnificent dragon that always roiled and shimmied down the street at the end of each Chinese New Year parade. The day had been challenging and frustrating, but I was so thankful for the awesomely beautiful sights.

Overall the day turned out fine, but on the way home up Highway 101, we discussed making t-shirts emblazoned with "I Survived the Dragon Parade." Events of the day truly seemed like a metaphor for my ability to be resourceful and survive what Jim and I would go through. To this day, my friends and I laugh when we recount the crazy twists and turns of our big-city Chinatown adventure. It is never lost on any of us what it meant to me to have their support for that day and every day since.

PROCESSING TREATMENT OPTIONS

Occasionally, Dr. Hardy would have information about trials and other treatment options he would discuss with us. Once or twice I made calls to inquire about trials, but our distance or the specifics of Jim's case always seemed to render him ineligible. Around April 2012, Dr. Hardy relayed that his former colleagues at Stanford had achieved some degree of success with a surgery for mesothelioma patients. With our approval, he called to ask if Jim could be seen. The following day, a Friday, Stanford called and advised us of an appointment the very next Monday morning. They went through a litany of questions on the telephone and sent us some papers to fill out. We were somewhat awed and encouraged that perhaps we need not give up all hope.

We made the uplifting two-and-a-half-hour drive to Stanford on Monday with CDs and reports in hand. The Golden Gate Bridge looked wondrous that day and we chatted happily along Highway 101 through San Francisco and transferring onto 280 South for the last leg of the trip to Stanford. All the while, a little voice in my head repeated "quality of life, quality of life" as I decided to reserve unbridled enthusiasm.

Arriving at Stanford Hospital, we were escorted to a room where five doctors met us at the same time. The level of attention Jim received was far beyond our expectations. They were very interested in his case and were thorough in their evaluation exam. Questions were many and wide-ranging. Whereas rapid response and interest from physicians to date had made us concerned, we left this special medical appointment feeling there might be possibilities to improve on Jim's situation.

By Thursday of that week, we were once again discouraged to learn that Jim was not a candidate for the procedure at Stanford. Given that his disease was so far along, the surgery the Stanford team had perfected was not expected to be successful for Jim. They declined to consider him further, with regrets.

The depths of our disappointment were such that another suggestion was not especially comforting. The Stanford doctors and Dr. Hardy talked further and agreed they would support a recommendation to consult with another surgeon at University of California San Diego who had gained considerable renown with a completely different surgical treatment for mesothelioma patients. It was an especially aggressive approach, but had succeeded in extending the lives of some patients by several precious years. Despite the enormous scope of this particular surgical procedure, which the

UC surgeon had helped develop, Jim wanted to look into it because he thought he might otherwise die by Christmas.

Again, I thought of Dr. Hanna's advice to keep quality of life in mind. The recovery from the surgery, even on a much younger person, was generally lengthy and difficult. When I mentioned this to Jim to make sure he was aware, he responded somewhat angrily that he felt the need to try. It was painful for me to watch Jim go through the ups and downs, discovering and discarding options, but he wanted me to make arrangements for a trip to UC San Diego and I wanted him to have all the answers he needed to make his decisions.

A WILD GETAWAY

On June 13, 2012, during a good part of his chemo cycle, Jim decided we should spend a night at a local tourist attraction we had been curious about for some time. I had been to Safari West for a dinner and short walking tour with a non-profit group some years before, but had never had the full "glamping" and Jeep tour experience. Safari West provides rescued African game animals with a safe outdoor environment and provides several levels of experiences with the animals as a way to raise money for their upkeep. We would sleep overnight in a sort of tent/ cabin hybrid and take a Jeep tour to the back of the property the next day.

A staff person brought our things to the tent, a short walk on a slight incline that I noticed was more challenging to Jim than either of us expected. Our quarters were absolutely lovely—rugged but beautiful. The porch of our cabin had a clear view of the giraffe area. Inside were all the comforts of home. Flowers, lovely beds, and furnishings. The "windows" were screens with roll-down canvas shades to help keep cold and wind out at night; the walls were canvas, too. The bathroom was open mesh at the top, beneath the eaves of the roof. There were heaters and the hot water came to the sink much faster than at our home. In addition to room heaters, the beds had electric blankets.

That evening we ate a simple meal in the main dining room and I took a little walk around the small animal enclosures. Jim sat on a bench, not feeling up to walking. I took lots of pictures on my phone to show him, including a picture of two flamingoes whose necks formed a perfect heart. Back at our tent, we watched giraffes necking sweetly from the porch until it became chilly and they were taken to their covered enclosures. All around us were exotic bird calls and monkey shrieks in the distance. I had brought along a favorite book, Gary Zukav's *The Seat of the Soul,* which I planned to read again after Jim fell asleep.

Quite suddenly, as we were preparing for bed, Jim took ill. He was extremely anxious and in pain. When questioned about the source of his stomach pain, his answers were expressions of alarm and panic, but not helpful. Up until this point, he had not experienced distress after eating, so I considered that as low on the list of possible causes of his discomfort. He seemed so anxious and upset that I wondered if he was having a panic attack and asked him if he wanted to go to the hospital.

"We can go home or I can take you to the hospital," I said as calmly as possible. "I'm OK with either one, and you don't have to worry about ruining this trip for me."

Jim insisted he did not want to leave.

"It's OK, sweetheart. I am here for whatever you need to do. Try to think about what you need, not me," I said.

He was not being comforted and calmed, so I sat on the bed alongside him and spoke softly. I asked him to think about what was worrying him and to consider that it might feel better if he talked about it. He decided he wanted to write a letter to his daughters. I had no paper but found a pen in the bottom of my purse. Jim began dictating to me as I removed the paper cover from my book and began to write on the inside of it in my own version of shorthand. Clearly emotional myself at the time, I have difficulty making out what I wrote. What he had to say reflected his state of mind in those moments:

"I wanted to write something [for] my family. I am of sound mind but my body is shot. People say I don't look sick, but they don't know what's going on inside. I've probably lost 80 percent of my strength. I can't walk fifty feet without getting tired. I've made it almost to my seventieth birthday. I want my family to know I love them very much. If I had it to do over again, I would go to that school, 'How to raise a family and be a better person.' I especially want Renee and Roberta to know I love them very much. I must have done something right because they turned out pretty good. I'm disappointed I won't be around for more barbecues and camping trips and other things I cherished in life.

A few words to my grandchildren: Derek, you'll be OK as soon as you settle down. At twenty-one, you have the potential to do something very worthwhile. Jack and Ella, I love you and wish we had more time together. For all of you, as you go down the path of life, I have two pieces of advice: Before making any decision, ask yourself first if it will hurt anyone, or will it embarrass [your] parents if they read about it in the newspaper . . ."

This was as far as Jim got with his rambling letter that night. Just talking and getting his worries and thoughts out seemed to help him. I wondered if his physical challenge on the small incline to the tent had upset him and contributed to his worry that his end-time was near. I set my notes aside and we just talked and held hands for a few minutes. Then we focused on guessing the calls of the birds and animals that could be heard. When we heard a jaguar let out a frighteningly loud shriek, we both looked at one another and laughed. Jim was now relaxed and said he no longer had pain. After he drifted off to sleep, I lay awake for a time listening to the animals and praying. It was a very cold night, but we were snug because there were space heaters, electric blankets, and every comfort. We both slept the entire night and awoke well rested and in good spirits.

After breakfast in the large dining area, we lined up for the Jeep tour. Knowing we would be on a rutted road and how upset Jim would become with me for not dodging manhole covers when I drove, I was worried Jim might have a problem and that an entire load of people might have their tour disrupted. Believing Jim might have had a panic attack the night before, I did not want to mention my concerns and put any ideas in his head about discomfort. Once I figured out which driver was ours, I took him aside and explained that my husband could not withstand much jostling due to his illness. The driver suggested we sit up front with him as that would be less bumpy. For most of the tour, which was fun and fascinating, our driver took the ruts and potholes carefully and we all had a great time. The herd animals—zebras, gnus, Cape buffalo, and antelope—stood placidly as we passed by. An ostrich showed too much interest in

Jim and had to be shooed away by the driver. Toward the end of the tour, a couple of children in the seats over our heads begged for the driver to take a few bumps faster. Jim gave him the go ahead and we all joined the kids in yelling and enjoying the thrill. He was none the worse for wear after the thrill ride.

Though I twice mentioned to Jim about finishing the letter he started, he decided he did not want to do so. Once this crisis had passed, he did not seem to feel it as urgent that he communicate his concerns in the immediate future. He would later handle what he had to say to family members in person, when the time felt right for him.

THE MEDICAL ROLLER-COASTER RIDE

"You will love San Diego. You should make it like a little honeymoon," a couple of different friends suggested.

This was one of those instances when I struggled to keep my cool and not shout, "Oh, shut up!"

Even before he was known to be sick, painful and personal losses began piling up for both of us, invisible to others. Couldn't people see how much we were struggling? Were we such good actors? This was Jim's life-and-death matter, not a movie. Despite action movie actors being beat to a pulp, there always seems to be an obligatory moment of passion for the lead characters. Our circumstances had beaten us both pretty badly, too, in ways not known to our friends and family. By this time, I firmly believed the disease was the major factor in my husband's somewhat sudden onset of impotence about eighteen months prior. I had asked him to see his doctor when he began experiencing sexual dysfunction, but Jim was too mortified.

By the time Dr. Hardy asked about sex at our first meeting, Jim still could not tell the truth, and I decided on the spot to take my cue from his choices.

It felt callous that others expected we were able to be physically romantic given Jim's discomfort and weakness from chemotherapy and draining of fluid that regularly poked holes in his abdomen. They knew nothing of his mortifying manly loss of ability. To cover, I smiled wanly and explained that we were going to be too busy with appointments in preparation for Jim's exploratory surgery to go sight-seeing or have much fun in San Diego. Besides, we would need to get back home for Jim's chemo and to our dogs, BD and Lily-Lou. We hated leaving our little buddies behind and always enjoyed coming home to them.

It was May when we left for San Diego on another expedition for hope. Before and during this trip, Jim and I often remarked how many exceptional and caring health care professionals we had encountered along the way. Like all the medical professionals we had seen before them, the staff and doctor at the UC San Diego Hospital could not have been more pleasant and welcoming. The surgeon was anxious to see how he could help. We didn't sleep too well awaiting the surgery, but were up at 5:00 a.m. to get Jim ready for the first surgery of the day. Once Jim went into surgery, I found a chair away from other family members in a great, open mezzanine. It was a beautiful hospital and this area felt like a place where I could lose myself for a little while. I fell asleep sitting sideways on a padded bench until the surgeon found me.

Jim was still in the recovery room but the doctor wanted to share his findings first with me. We already knew that for Jim's age and the advances of his disease, such a surgery would be very challenging. If there were complications, he might not fully recover, and this could affect or even shorten his remaining time. Before the exploratory procedure, the surgeon explained that he hoped, if all went well with the major surgery under consideration, Jim's life could possibly be extended by about two years. However, once inside to look at the tissues, the doctor found the disease had begun to invade in ways that made the surgery inadvisable. The cancer had affected the mesentery, the layer of connective tissue that covers different organs in the abdomen, and attached to another organ, elevating concern and closing the door on this option. Had he not found this new development, the surgeon still would have urged cautious consideration due to the scope of the procedure. As concerned as I had been about the scope of the surgery, I was equally worried about Jim's response to this latest bit of bad news.

Being present for Jim as he took in the information this surgeon had to share was one of the hardest things I ever had to do as a wife. We had experienced several months of ups and downs: renewed hope followed by despair. The trip to San Diego was, I believed, the final frontier for miracle procedures that could possibly extend Jim's life unless the oncologist discovered a miracle chemical mixture or clinical trial in short order. On some level, though the news was not good and it eliminated what we thought was surely the last of Jim's options, I felt some relief to have the answer. Dr. Hanna's "think quality of life" had become a refrain that played often in my head. I did not want to see Jim lose out on "good time" because of a surgery that might not significantly extend or improve his situation.

The resignation on Jim's face as the doctor's explanation sunk in was something so foreign to an upbeat person of good humor. It signaled to me that we were now on the same sad page. I expected the trip home to be dismal. True to his nature, however, Jim managed somehow to set his worry aside and to pay attention to life around him. Concerns I had previously kept to myself, I now shared with him. Doing so seemed, at that point in time, to serve as reinforcement to him that the surgery was not for him. Jim decided to focus on his chemotherapy and to worry less about how much time he had. He still was relatively strong, so he still felt there was time to enjoy life.

FINDING OUR NEW NORMAL

Jim had to give up on his part-time job once chemo started, but he now doubled down his efforts to golf and spend time with his friends. There were days when he did not feel up to it, but he remained more or less vital and active. Overall, he looked good. Mid-week poker games with his friends were a highlight. His friends took an active interest in brightening his days and inviting him to things they thought he would enjoy. We worked around the pattern of good and bad days to make plans for little trips. Jim occasionally talked of wanting to do things that I knew were beyond his abilities, but I learned to let him talk. I had always urged him to take the guided hunting trip on horseback that he occasionally spoke of since I had known him. Now when he brought it up, I just listened. Not only had his health rendered it unfeasible, the friends he wanted to share the experience with were now too old and would not go. He hunted and fished with his brother whenever he could. He kept up the yard work at a slower pace, working in stages and determined to see each task through.

The chemotherapy sessions seemed to be keeping the disease at bay, or at least slowing it. However, Jim's mid-section was now tender from the slender tubes inserted into him to alleviate the discomfort of excess fluid. We did things that we had not done together before and tried to include loved ones. A trip to San Francisco to see a baseball game with Jim's brother and sister-in-law, Dennis and Karen, was a highlight.

As friends of family were told of his fatal disease, it became somewhat uncomfortable to receive what some thought of as appropriate expressions of sympathy in Jim's presence. At one party, a guest I barely knew seemed unable to stop hugging and touching me. An initial hug and knowing look would have been sufficient. We were at the party to have a good time and the constant reminder was frankly annoying. There was another woman who would stick her lower lip out and make a childish frowny face when she talked with me.

Another issue that required delicate handling was the medical advice from well-meaning friends who lacked medical degrees. Some seemed to think cannabis was a cure for anything. Others seemed to think all terminal cancer diagnoses are treated in the same way and have the same effects. The worst were those who told us how their loved ones had died. Over time, these displays of too much pity, too much advice, and too much information caused us to begin closing ranks to spend time only with those who knew us best and understood that being treated as normal was Jim's greatest wish. We would also go off on our own for changes of scenery. Jim was soon no longer interested in meeting new people or in receiving misguided advice regarding his treatment, so it could be difficult for well-meaning friends to understand why Jim was not interested in attending large events and celebrations that did not focus on his family.

BURYING JIM'S PARENTS

After making a call to the local funeral home, Jim announced to me that he had an appointment to make his burial arrangements. Being turned down when I volunteered to join him was not a surprise. Jim was emphatic about doing things on his own whenever possible. It seemed almost unnecessarily brave, but I was thankful he was not in denial and was doing his best to cope and not avoid the important planning details. As he did each of these things, Jim would bring them up in discussion with his friends at their weekly outings. I think they marveled at how he confronted the reality of his impending end of life.

The funeral director told Jim about the Sacramento Valley National Cemetery in Dixon, California and about the benefits afforded to veterans. He helped Jim with the paperwork and Jim asked about burying his parents there. Jim's parents had passed away in 2007 and 2009 and we had their cremains at our home, not sure what to do with them. Since Jim's dad, Walt, had served in the US Army, they were eligible to be buried at Dixon, a new VA cemetery.

The military detail and personnel operating the cemetery were respectful and helpful when we made the arrangements for Jim's parents, a joint burial in July 2012. The service for Jim's dad was simple and very touching, so Jim was pleased to have discovered this option for them, as well as for himself. Most of us had long ago dealt with our grief over his parents' passing, but we found ourselves very emotional at the service, just the same. We all knew we would return someday soon to say goodbye to Jim. As we departed, Jim's brother, Dennis, told me he heard Jim say to his parents that he would "see them soon."

GOODBYES AND GIFTS

Jim began going through his desk and garage storage to make lists of what he wanted to give away and to whom. His idea of what was meaningful and valuable was different than that of his children, but I urged them to gratefully accept whatever he wanted them to have. They could do whatever they wanted later, but I felt it important to help him unburden himself. The grandchildren were not quite sure what to think of the trinkets he had collected for them and forgotten to give them when they were younger, but they graciously accepted the gifts during their visits.

As more time passed, I noticed Jim was becoming thinner and his weight was the subject of confusion for him. He could see his arms and legs getting thinner, but was confused that the scales did not show much weight loss. I did not want to force an image on him of the cancer mass growing in his body and the ongoing ascites accumulation, so I tried to gently explain that his middle was still large. Like my father, Jim formerly had large workman's hands that were rough and calloused. I always thought of them as strong and manly. My father's hands had become soft when he retired from his work as an electrician and slender as his illness gradually took him. Now Jim's hands had taken on the same softness as he was less active, and they too were thinning.

In August of 2012, we were invited to take a trip to the Mendocino coast with Jim's long-time friends, Paul and Carol. It would be an easy trip and they were amenable to pacing things for Jim, who was walking slower and shorter distances now. Sadly, less than a week before that trip, our beloved poodle suffered a seizure and we were devastated to see the damage it had done. We went to the vet right away and brought BD home to see how he would progress. It was quickly clear that BD was unlikely to improve. We talked again with the vet, who did a few more tests. We could spend a great deal of money and put the dog through a great deal of added stress with no assurance he would improve. When the vet demonstrated the extent of BD's new disabilities to us and said he could not promise BD was pain-free, I knew a tough decision was needed. This sad decision was everything other pet owners experience, but also urgent because Jim's needs were so great and required my full attention.

I felt guilty, but the idea of trying to make room in my caregiving schedule for BD when Jim's needs now consumed my full day was untenable. BD had been mine since just after my father passed away. Jim and I both thought he would be around to cushion the blow of Jim's passing, but it was not to be. Jim was too sensitive to participate in the decision but I would do anything to assure my little friend would not suffer. Jim accompanied me when I decided to put BD down, but he was so overcome he had to leave the veterinarian's office. BD received his shot and I held him until he was gone. I had to ask the staff to take him away so I could go to Jim.

I tried not to dwell on the loss, but we both succumbed to tears several times over the course of a week or two. Fortunately, we were going out of town in a day or so with Paul and Carol. Lily-Lou, my little rescue Chihuahua, would stay at King's Kastle, where she and BD often had gone together. Paul and Carol understood losing BD came at a terrible time and were very understanding as we did our best to focus on the fun of the trip. Jim needed to rest quite a lot, so Carol and I would go off to walk and talk, leaving our husbands to sit in the garden recalling old hunting and fishing stories, as well as to talk frankly about life.

Upon returning home we were happy to have Lily-Lou on the job, wagging and enthusiastically greeting us. Jim had been unhappy when I unexpectedly brought her home from the Humane Society at eight weeks old in March of 2011, but he had eventually developed a grudging acceptance. Within a couple weeks of BD's passing, Jim commented that he thought having her was a good thing. Translation: I've fallen in love with the little stinker. At first Lily seemed to miss her playmate, BD. Then it seemed as though she liked having all the attention to herself. Jim began to appreciate her personality and their mutual neediness seemed like a good thing. She snuggled with him every time he sat down. She took BD's place in a chair next to Jim on the front porch when he would sit outside for fresh air. I would watch them through the kitchen window as they became closer. We grieved the loss of BD, but Lily earned our love for what she contributed to our family during the tough times.

REASONS TO CELEBRATE THE DIAGNOSTIC ANNIVERSARY

As the summer months of 2012 slipped into the past, we became mindful of what the doctor had told us when Jim first asked how long he might live. Celebrating Christmas together again looked like a sure thing as Jim seemed to be well-maintained with the chemotherapy and other procedures that kept him comfortable. His energy level was cyclical during chemotherapy and he sometimes had difficulty keeping a meal down, but those seemed minor compared to other cancer patients we had heard about. Overall, Jim could still maintain most of his preferred past-times if he did not squander his energy on too much work around the house. He did not like for me to remind him to rest up for something he would be doing later, preferring instead to find the limits of his abilities on his own, even if he blew it occasionally.

One thing that concerned me the first year was that we did not see as much of his daughters as we would have liked. Jim and I seemed to initiate most family gatherings. It wasn't up to me to push them into visiting, but I did occasionally encourage them to do so when I was giving them updates on his condition. However, I later figured out that Jim's conversations with them were so positive they may have formed a different impression of his situation that allowed them to deny his terminal status or to suspect me of being overly dramatic. When we were together around the holidays, I listened to Jim's description of his health status when he talked to others and found it to be overly optimistic. It could have been an effort to avoid pity, or perhaps he really forgot the bad days when he was in the midst of good ones. We both knew he had numerous bad days and discomfort, but he seldom brought bad days up, even to the doctor. And he certainly did not want to be reminded of negative things when he was enjoying himself.

When our versions of Jim's status didn't match up, his daughters weren't sure whom to believe. Eventually, unless I felt something had to be shared with them right away, I learned to wait for them to ask me questions in private before sharing what I knew, and I tried always to relay only what the doctor had told us rather than to put my own spin on it. We were setting up to have a joyful Christmas, and I wondered if the doctor had not been deliberately conservative so we could fully appreciate Christmas 2012. Either way, the blessing was lost on no one. And when the family celebration was over, Jim and

I were happy to quietly enjoy the comforts of home and our little pooch by the fireplace.

THE OPTION OF PALLIATIVE CARE

Had Jim and Paula inquired further about palliative care, he could have requested a palliative care consultation once he received his diagnosis. Palliative care doctors can be part of multidisciplinary teams of social workers, pharmacists, nutritionists, and nurses in medical centers that coordinate care with the patient's oncologist. Or, in small communities they are doctors who focus on treating the symptoms and spiritual/emotional responses from serious diseases in conjunction with the treating physicians. Palliative care is covered by many insurances and Medicare. It gives the person with serious or terminal illness many layers of needed support. They may make recommendations to the primary doctor or oncologist about management of pain, nausea, fatigue, depression. and many other symptoms. They continue support from the beginning of the disease through end of life, providing comforting consistency. Though Paula and Jim dealt with Jim's course of disease relatively capably, palliative care doctors could have helped Jim prepare for most of the forks in the road and would have partnered with him to help decide when to stop treatment. And, they would have been supportive to Paula and his family, helping Paula better cope with the twists and turns of his care needs.

CHAPTER SUMMARY

- During the fact-finding portion of the diagnosis process, patients often prefer to keep the sharing of information limited to those who need to know. It may also be best to save revealing the bad news of a terminal diagnosis for a time when more complete information can be provided.
- The best advice we received during the darkest of times was to consider quality of life above extraordinary life-extending measures that could negatively impact Jim's remaining lifespan or even shorten it.
- Caregiving stress is real and doesn't always require a long time to become evident. Caregivers are urged to have a relationship with a health care provider who is aware of their circumstances so changes in their stress and well-being, including sleep disruptions and depression, can be addressed in a timely manner.
- Despite the bad news of a terminal diagnosis, immediate attention to financial planning, addressing legal matters, and planning for one's burial can provide tremendous comfort to the terminal patient and the family.
- A positive caregiver outlook is reassuring to the patient. At the same time, being comfortable with caregiving and facing the challenges of the job provide tremendous personal growth for caregivers who are up to the emotional and physical demands.

- The ups and downs of the early exploration of a cancer patient's options are sometimes a stressful roller coaster ride of hope and disappointment as health care providers research options. For us, once the terrain leveled out it became easier to appreciate less eventful days that allowed us to live more normally.
- Unsolicited advice from friends about medications and treatments can be misleading, or even upsetting. Patience helps when unsolicited advice is given by well-meaning individuals. The types of cancer treatments and methods are up to the physician and patient based on treatment goals and specifics of the patient's condition. New treatments regularly become available.
- Palliative care physicians are covered by Medicare and work with a multi-disciplinary team and coordinate with a patient's primary doctor or oncologist to manage the patient's symptoms during care and to help with decisions such as when to stop treatment. Patients who request palliative care enjoy consistent attention to their symptoms, including depression, through end of life. Both patient and family benefit from an ongoing extra layer of support.

Resources

www.palliativedoctors.org/start/resources

Chapter Four

LIVING

FRIENDS

Throughout Jim's remaining life, we were able to enjoy good times and brief respites from the terrible reality. The 2013 joint birthday celebration Jim shared with his youngest daughter was more joyful than the previous year when the family was reeling from the first news of the diagnosis. This time we celebrated that Jim had survived beyond the first Christmas since his diagnosis and that he was still fairly strong. Jim and I could acknowledge there were more challenges to come, but we appreciated each day when we could respond to friendly inquiries that there was really nothing new and Jim was doing rather well.

Jim's weight and vitality had decreased somewhat from a year ago, but he was still independently mobile and able to participate in some of his favorite activities. We scheduled little outings or short trips for the days Jim was feeling best. Sometimes our friends would come up with ideas for pleasant distractions, thoughtfully keeping Jim's needs in mind. Following the ups and downs of our Dragon

Year, I was delighted to give my best friend a green light to fly out from Chicago for a visit.

Janine and I have been close since our early twenties, when we worked together for a corporate hotel and restaurant firm based in Washington, DC. Having supported one another through many of life's trials, we had long ago come to think of our relationship as more like sisters than friends. Her birthday being within a couple days of Jim's, Janine could not resist coming out to visit with us and to spend some time with him. Janine first met Jim in 1994 when she brought her mother out to California for a visit. Both liked him very much and Jim quickly became fond of them as we hauled them around to see the sights of Northern California and the San Francisco Bay Area.

Margo, Janine's mother, had flirty eyes and a sultry voice. A widow, she openly flirted with Jim when we went out to dinner. Janine and I snickered as we watched Margo dance with Jim and flirt until his face glowed red. A former showgirl, Margo later sent Jim a glossy publicity photo from her show business career with a saucy inscription. As a joke, I took a black and white photo of Jim dressed as a bare-chested comic version of an Errol Flynn pirate. He signed it with a Sharpie and we mailed that back to Margo: "Love, Jim."

Having Janine around is always fun because she is my most spontaneously silly friend. God love her, she is capable of lifting my mood even when I think I don't want it lifted. During the visit in 2013, upon learning I had an unavoidable business commitment one evening, Janine insisted Jim take her out for a birthday dinner. They went to one of our local restaurants and Janine promised him tongues would wag in our small town afterward. They had a lot of fun that night and she mischievously gave Jim a big kiss in the middle of the restaurant to let him know how much she loved him. Though she was in regular contact with us throughout the remainder of his life (and beyond, of course), I am happy she visited at that time. Janine often recalls how special that evening was for her. Good friends and good memories are essential to a good life. That's how I know my life has been very, very good.

CHANGE ON THE WAY

Early in 2013, there was a shift in the trajectory of Jim's journey. We had enjoyed the somewhat routine treatment period between March 2012 and January 2013. By late January, Jim opened up to me about his desire to stop chemo after nearly a year of treatment. He didn't feel it was working and believed it was a waste of resources for him to continue accepting treatment. Again, though I knew it was his decision, I longed to hold on to the uneventfulness a bit longer and feared dropping treatment would expedite changes I did not want. I referred to the first year of my journey with Jim as The Dragon Year, with ups and downs, ins and outs, hope and disappointment. The idea of his stopping chemo scared the hell out of me. Though I could see Jim's decline each month, it had been slower than I originally thought it might be. Jim discussed quitting chemo with Dr. Hardy. He ultimately decided to finish the current cycle after which he and Dr. Hardy would then revisit the idea of stopping treatment.

Around this time, we arranged a short trip during the best part of the chemo cycle. Jim had long been curious about the snow train from the Bay Area to Reno. It was supposed to be entertaining and the sights along the way quite beautiful. We booked the upper "glass" level of the car and enjoyed an elegant lunch on the way into the wintry, picturesque Sierra Nevada.

When we arrived in Reno at the train stop below street level, it was not immediately clear to us which direction would take us to our hotel. It was freezing cold and Jim was very tired from the trip. We had two heavy suitcases on wheels and the altitude was not helping Jim's energy level. He became upset and cranky when I could not immediately figure out the direction we should walk. It was a matter of a couple blocks, but to Jim it seemed like a marathon. He was irritable because he was panicked that he might not make it to the hotel without collapsing. At the same time, his pride stood in the way of allowing me to drag both of suitcases behind me. It appeared our plan for a nice trip was falling apart.

Desperate to solve the problem and protect his pride, I tried to convince Jim to stay in place so I could look for a solution, ideally an alternative to walking. He was too upset and outside his comfort zone to cooperate but it was impossible to be angry with my husband who was normally so cooperative. This was my first heads-up to do a better job planning something unfamiliar by asking for more details in advance.

Somehow, we did make it to the hotel on foot and Jim rested for a time so we could enjoy our familiar Reno routine. Throughout our marriage, Reno had been a twice-yearly getaway, so we enjoyed our time in the casino and taking in a show. We ate light meals as his appetite had shrunk but it was a pleasant time overall, made somewhat bittersweet as I wondered if this would be our last visit there together. Jim posed for a picture with showgirls (again, the showgirl thing) from the casino show that makes me grin whenever I look at it. What a ham!

On the way home, we gazed down the mountainside from our train at Donner Lake that was half frozen. We slid in and out of tunnels as snowflakes came down harder and grew bigger, a delightful sight from the safety of the train. Having learned my lesson about planning, I formulated a plan to get from the train to the car without mishap, explaining the plan to Jim long before we arrived back at the Bay Area train station. We were already familiar with that station and Jim was not worried about unknowns, so all went smoothly. Like choosing when to offer advice or share new information, I was learning to choose my timing to help Jim to accept accommodation as his needs increased.

GOOD DAYS, BAD DAYS

Around March 2013, Jim completed his chemotherapy cycle and did not return to it. He was tired of spending so much time in the chemo chair and the endless blood tests. By then, I had become resigned to his decision. In my heart, I knew if he didn't make the decision, some incident would force it on him later. Perhaps for him, it was better to call his own shots. Jim would still return to the hospital to have fluid drained as needed, but the decision to cease chemotherapy seemed to help him regain a certain amount of freedom, personal time, and normalcy.

The first idea Jim had for a special outing after the end of chemotherapy was an afternoon of horseback riding with his children and grandchildren. This was not going to be a rigorous trip for an average person, but rather a loping trail ride. The family was as puzzled I was regarding this choice of entertainment, but I asked them to bear with Dad, who loved western movies. One member of the party was a bit nervous about a first encounter with a horse, but went along without complaint. Jim did not offer any information about his condition, so I had to take the guide aside and explain the situation. Outside his hearing range we agreed the ride would end if Jim experienced any difficulties.

I stayed behind to set up a gourmet picnic for the family to enjoy when the ride was over. When they returned, we spent a good deal of time taking photos of everyone on their horses. I walked over to Jim and he quietly begged me to help him off the horse. Jim was so exhausted and limp I was afraid he might fall, so I called the guide over to assist. We enjoyed lunch in the picnic area before heading home. Jim seemed quite pleased with the day, so I was appreciative the family came together to make a special day for their father and grandpa.

Around the beginning of May, as our anniversary approached, Jim wanted to buy me something special. I had been admiring a piece of jewelry, so we went to the jeweler one morning. A born negotiator, Jim went off to rest in a chair after reaching what he thought was a good price adjustment with the jeweler. I handled signing for the purchase as Jim was definitely losing ground in terms of his stamina.

A day or two later, we went to an anniversary dinner and enjoyed a celebratory drink, though Jim had mostly given up drinking. I watched in amazement as he ate a large meal of calamari steak accompanied by heavily seasoned side dishes that smelled too rich for my taste. He had always loved eating so I wanted to be happy he was enjoying this meal. I had learned not to rain on Jim's parade by saying anything, but by the time the check arrived Jim realized he had seriously crossed a line.

Suddenly very uncomfortable, he was in a hurry to leave and we couldn't leave the restaurant quickly enough. We were just about three blocks from the restaurant when Jim urgently shouted for me to pull over. I did so as quickly as I could. Jim opened the car door and I don't need to describe further what happened. He was mortified and angry because he thought I had not pulled over fast enough and he had wasted a good meal. He fumed, grousing through a litany of complaints as he dealt with his embarrassment and discomfort. He didn't want someone to think he had drunk too much and hoped nobody had seen the incident. It also bothered him to have messed up the street and then driven away. I assured him he was not to the first to be sick on the street and it was more important to get him home. To this point in time, Jim had experienced very little vomiting, so I chalked it up to too much rich food and maybe the drink. He felt better after being sick but the emotional upset at the loss of his formerly hearty appetite stayed with him for some time.

Throughout this caregiving phase, I maintained a couple activities to give myself a break and allow me to relax. Lunch or tea with friends was something that could be done on the spur of the moment. Sometimes a movie. A new friend, Diane, was a wonderful listener and conversationalist. After unburdening myself, our talks were far-ranging over many topics of interest and I always looked forward to time with Diane and dog walks with Antonella on a regular basis to maintain my emotional equilibrium.

Every six weeks I went to have a pedicure at my favorite spa. It was a fairly long drive but I preferred this spa because the service was luxurious and performed in privacy and quiet, unlike other places where customers were all getting services and chatting loudly in the same room. There were times when I could almost levitate because

I was so relaxed, and other times when I would grieve by crying silently while the service provider brought relief to my aching feet. Jim had no objection to my pedicures, but was curious why I would drive more than thirty miles when pedicures could be had much closer. So, I booked us an appointment together.

When we arrived, Jim thought the spa music sounded like something played in a funeral home. "That's because they want customers to feel as though they have died and gone to heaven," I joked.

We had our respective pedicures after which I asked Jim if he understood why I made the effort to go to that place. He agreed it was a most relaxing experience. Later, when he became more frail, I had to ask someone to be with him so I could be gone for two hours to the spa. Our friend, Lori, agreed to stay with Jim. She has a sassy sense of humor and is a natural caregiver. The two of them enjoyed trading barbs. When I asked Jim if he needed me to help him to the restroom before I departed, a devilish grin appeared on his face.

"No, Lori can handle that."

We all had a good laugh. Lori later told me that after she read the newspaper, he insisted that she refold it as it had been folded when delivered. Jim was a stickler for that with me, but I was a little embarrassed he had done that with her. She found it funny and dished right back at him, so their time together was a pleasant departure from people tip-toeing around and making Jim feel pitied.

When Jim's youngest daughter, Roberta, and her spouse invited us to join them and the grandchildren at a friend's vacation home at Lake Tahoe, we eagerly accepted the invitation to have a couple days with them. It was a very relaxing time in that we mostly talked, shared meals, and enjoyed the children. We played silly games and laughed with the children over a game of telephone where whispered messages became hilariously convoluted. Roberta and her husband cooked wonderful meals. Mixed drinks flowed during cocktail time, of which Jim drank probably three that first night. My gentle suggestion that alcohol could be a problem was seen as an attempt to ruin his good time. I had long ago gotten over feeling sensitive about Jim's angry outbursts or dismissals of my concern. It didn't happen often and I was convinced it was his way of coping or feeling in charge.

Jim went to bed fairly early that night and the rest of us stayed up talking. Roberta had questions about her father's disease and how he was doing, so I shared the latest information we had from his health care team. There were tears and memories that seemed important to share. That night, shortly after I went to bed, Jim was up sick. We spent most of the night up together as I tried to help him.

The next day was the same as the first, good and bad in the same ways. Despite being so sick the night before, Jim wanted to enjoy alcohol and I knew we would have another sleepless night. I wondered if he just was not convinced as to the cause of his night sickness, but he surely was convinced the second night. To say the least, I was exhausted after two nights of being up with him through his misery. Under normal circumstances, especially since I had to drive us home despite my lack of sleep, I would have been justified letting my husband suffer for drinking too much. Now I could not help but feel I should enjoy him not just when he was sweet, but to remember I would soon not have the luxury of thinking of him as a jackass for ignoring my sensible advice. It was better in my mind to sit up and comfort him than to be righteous about his choices.

MAKING THE BEST CHOICES TO SUPPORT DAILY COMFORT

Jim was a relatively cooperative care recipient. Still, it can be challenging for spouses when their good advice is disregarded, as Jim disregarded Paula's suggestion about drinking during their family visit. In this case, she had no choice but to allow Jim to find his own boundaries. However, had Jim been followed by a palliative care doctor, he may have been able to consult with a nutritionist who would have advised (and likely convinced) him about food and beverage choices and their consequences given his cancer condition. The accumulation of ascites fluid indicated that Jim had tumors in his gastro-intestinal system, so his liver had lost the ability to metabolize alcohol normally. The nutritionist would have warned him in the early stage of his disease of the unpleasant consequences from alcohol ingestion. Had he understood why he could not tolerate alcohol and that he would vomit it up, he might have been considerably less inclined to consume it and could have bypassed the suffering during his trip to Lake Tahoe.

THE BIG SHIFT

"Honey," I began when he shuffled from the bathroom and sat at the table after being sick yet again at night.

"1 feel like something has changed for you and I am out of tools to make you feel better when you are so sick." I paused before proceeding. "Do you think it's time to call hospice?"

"Yes. Call."

* * *

The trip to Tahoe was just a week or so past when Jim again began waking up at night in considerable distress, vomiting in response to a painful gut. Now at home, he was not drinking alcohol, nor was he over-eating, but after three really bad nights in less than a week, I wondered if his illness had crossed a critical threshold. I could see he was dispirited and weak. I spent a difficult day wrestling with what I could do to help. It had been seventeen months since we first went to Dr. Rutherford's office to find out why Jim's stomach had grown so distended. Now we were well past the time Dr. Hardy first suggested might be "a good long time" for Jim to live past his diagnosis.

He was resting comfortably, but would get up soon. It seemed odd, but I once again looked for a way to frame a difficult question when Jim was at a low point. His upbeat periods were never the time to bring up difficult things. Perhaps because a solution to his discomfort or upset was needed, Jim was better able to consider and accept hard ideas and suggestions when he was in a hard place. I had to make the suggestion this day because it was Friday and the weekend loomed ahead. And yes, it was partly selfish. I could not bear to see him suffer.

As startling as it was to hear his response, I knew considering hospice was the right thing and acted quickly on his request. After all, if we were wrong, we'd find out. I called Dr. Hardy and had a brief conversation. He did not hesitate and said he would call hospice right away.

The hospice representative called within the hour and we had a meeting in the living room about two hours after that. A social worker and intake nurse were our first contacts. As scary as it was to acknowledge what was happening, the hospice professionals were compassionate, thorough, and organized. We found that comforting.

They said they would check in on the next day, Saturday, to make sure Jim wanted to proceed and they would set everything in motion to make him comfortable. They left with a thorough understanding of Jim's most immediate need for relief from pain and nausea. After they left, we cried and comforted one another, acknowledging this big and unavoidable step.

The next day we received a confirmation call and a visit from a nurse who phoned in the first prescription to keep Jim comfortable. This is when we became acquainted with Jo. She explained that morphine would be central to Jim's pain control. Surely, this is difficult for some families, but we both had some familiarity with the benefits of morphine during the dying process of other loved ones. I also knew from previous experiences that morphine is commonly used in emergency room situations because it works quickly.

Their father's admittance to hospice was sure to be a hard thing for Jim's daughters so I gathered hospice information booklets, including the easy-to-understand *Gone from my Sight*, for them to read. I provided them both with telephone numbers of the nurse and social worker. I encouraged them both to call and told them to feel free to do so at any time if they had questions about Jim's care and the methods we were following to help bring his life to a peaceful conclusion. Proactive Renee called right away and asked her questions.

The one surprise to me during the establishment of our partnership with hospice was the request that all of Jim's hunting guns be removed from the house. The suggestion was made away from Jim's hearing. Despite my protest that Jim seemed fairly well-adjusted, the social worker explained that some dying adults are very good at concealing their intentions to abruptly end their lives. I had already had one suicide experience in my life that verified this and Jim was still physically capable of doing so. Jim did not seem to be depressed beyond adjusting to his situation, but I decided this was a good time for me to start following the advice I had asked for.

Fortunately, Jim had once spoken of distributing his guns to his brother and others, so I made the suggestion that he do so now; he had already conceded he would no longer be able to hunt. I assured him it would be more enjoyable to give them away himself than to leave it to me later, since I didn't know one gun from another. When he agreed to distribute the guns to other family members, I called the girls and asked them to gratefully accept the gifts and to just hold onto them if they didn't want them. Uncle Dennis could take care of the guns for them later. Jim did insist I keep one handgun for my protection after he was gone. I hid it in a place he would never find it. My intent was to give it to Dennis later, but I hid it so well it took *me* a long time to find it! I am my mother's daughter. She used to hide our Christmas gifts so well we would often open a stray gift in April once her spring cleaning was underway.

Within a couple days of calling hospice, we knew it was the right thing to do at that time. They immediately got Jim's nausea and vomiting under control. Having our hospice team meant we could get questions answered; we had professionals on call day and night for help if we did not know what to do. And we no longer felt alone on this journey. Over a few weeks, Jim was introduced to a full complement of hospice services. He met with a chaplain, a volunteer visitor, and others who were appropriate at that time. He indicated what he liked and politely declined whatever service he did not find useful.

DECLINE AND DEVOTION

As one might expect, the advent of hospice in our lives coincided with a time of accelerated loss. Jim's friends continued to come for poker and I was pleased that he had all sorts of nice things to say to them about his initial hospice experience. He had been rendered unable to play a round of golf, which was a terrible and painful blow to his independence. He had begun sleeping more, but his closest friends were good about letting him talk and listening, more than I expect men normally do. They understood that poker was a highlight in Jim's world, even when he reached the point where his focus was slipping and he did not always understand who won.

By July, Jim spent most of his day in the easy chair in front of the television or sitting on the front porch with our Chihuahua, Lily-Lou. When he wanted to move from one place to another he required my help, especially to get over the step into and out of the house. Despite having a cane and walker, Jim was somewhat resistant to using them—I surmised that was a result of his fear of losing mobility.

Sometime into the hospice portion of Jim's journey, I found myself frequenting our local pharmacy as Jim's needs and condition changed quickly and often. Pharmacist Fred Besio and his staff were compassionate and went above and beyond to make sure we had everything needed when we needed it. It made me proud to live in a friendly, small community.

One day during this time when things seemed to be moving quickly, I began to feel pressure (self-imposed) to tell Jim how much he meant to me. I was not sure I had explicitly expressed my love for him or that he understood how much I appreciated our marriage and time together. It felt urgent that I do so while he could still take in what I was saying. The day finally arrived when I could no longer hold back on delivery of an impromptu speech of gratitude. I could not let Jim die without knowing the extent of my love.

The more I talked, the more emotional I became, assuring my plan would badly backfire. Jim became upset at my tears and asked me to stop and to not do that again. I felt terrible and was shocked into stopping and leaving the room to deal with my mortification. "How stupid," I thought. "He doesn't want to be reminded of my impending losses. I need to be mindful of making his time easier." I did not apologize and did not bring it up again. "This is about him, not me," I reminded myself. Making myself feel better would not help Jim, unless it was to feel good about doing the best caregiving job I could do. So I returned to that focus.

MANY GOODBYES

Jim continued to try to keep track of his checkbook and to monitor our finances, but it was becoming more difficult. He would show me how he wanted me to do things when he was gone, but I would have to sometimes help him with the math of balancing the checkbook, which upset him terribly.

Occasionally, he would decide to do something that seemed odd or out of the ordinary, obsessing until it was complete or he got his way. One hot summer afternoon, he decided it was urgent to install a license plate on the front of my car, which had no place for a plate to be installed. He was going to drill the bumper to install it. There were times when Jim had proven less than handy, so when I couldn't talk him out of it, I at least got his agreement he would be certain what was behind where he drilled. With so much going on, I could not deal with a hole in the radiator. Worse, I didn't want Jim to be injured or to get in trouble.

Jim's stamina was so compromised by this time, I watched him holding the handrail as he descended the front steps to the street. After crouching in front of the car he soon lay on the pavement in front of it as he became more tired. Fifteen minutes passed and he was struggling, unable to hold his arms up to work. I went outside to see if I could help, expecting him to be angry with me. Mentally noting there was an extra hole in the bumper, I helped him screw the license plate into place and helped him to sit up. We rested a bit and then I used all the strength I could muster to get him to his feet and help him into the house. Once in his lounge chair, Jim was so tired he cried in acknowledgement of his depleted strength. Each event of loss for Jim also felt like a loss for me, but I forced myself to be strong in front of him, though I often did have to dab my eyes in his presence.

One afternoon, I went downtown to take a little break and get out of the house for an hour. There was a little shop where I enjoyed browsing the new merchandise from time to time. As I chatted with the woman who ran the business, the subject came up of my husband being sick and she remarked that she hoped he would soon be well. I explained that Jim was on hospice care and was completely unprepared for her response.

"Oh, well then you don't have much longer," she said cheerfully while packaging up my purchase.

My hand went to my stomach. Had someone just kicked me there? I'm sure my mouth was hanging open and I remember being unable to speak because it felt as though the breath had been sucked out of me. She seemed unaware how her off-handed attempt to make me feel better had crash landed. I said nothing else as she chattered on until handing me the bag. I attempted to mutter some sort of farewell and dashed out of the store to my car for a cry.

For many months, Jim's beloved 1972 Chevy pickup truck sat covered in the garage. He finally decided we should place an ad on Craigslist and several potential buyers came to see him. The vehicle had served a major role in his hunting and fishing adventures, as well as some special camping outings we had enjoyed together. A nice young couple was very enthusiastic about the truck and did not attempt to get Jim to lower his asking price. They came with a trailer to haul the truck home and Jim seemed really pleased that his treasured vehicle would be in good hands and that they would restore it to its former beauty.

As he sat in the garage and watched them drive away, I put my hand on his shoulder. His stoic demeanor melted away as crushing grief overcame him. He waved his hand at me to go away. When I hesitated, he angrily said, "Go inside!"

Remembering we had gone on our first date in that vehicle, I wanted to cry, too. It broke my heart to leave Jim to sob alone. This was a strong man, my protector. Now he was vulnerable, and he still needed privacy from his most intimate confidant to grieve. I dared not force myself or my attempts to comfort on him. Comfort was all I had to give and that was useless in this moment.

One can only guess whether continued treatment would have postponed Jim's decline any longer, but I feel confident he was living as he wanted to once he decided to end treatment. He was not in denial about dying, so there were some sad times. However, he clearly made the most of good times. His doctors were compassionate, and I felt they would have eventually suggested the choice to end treatment to Jim if he had not made the decision on his own. After all, they are not required to give treatment that is not going to benefit the patient. For Jim, it seemed a healthy sign that he remained in charge of his choices.

Jim was leaving home less and less since going on hospice. It was very helpful when the hospice doctor came to the house to drain his ascites. Unexpectedly, I learned to assist with the paracentesis procedure as hospice physician Dr. Gary Johanson tended to Jim. Dr. Johanson had been on the leading edge of the hospice movement in this country. As busy as he was, he seemed to take all the time Jim needed, and Jim liked talking with him. The procedure was much more comfortable when Jim received it at home. Perhaps it was that he did not have the added strain of travel to the hospital, or just that the morphine played a role. With each step, we saw the many accommodations afforded by hospice making Jim more physically and emotionally comfortable and making my caregiving easier.

CELEBRATING

In early July Jim decided to have some sort of celebration with his friends and family in lieu of a large funeral. Rather than a post-mortem celebration of life, we chose a pre-death "Slice of Life" celebration to take place August 4. Invitations with upbeat images and text went out to about 120 friends of Jim's choosing. The food theme featured several of Jim's favorite types of pie. As it was unusual, a couple people responded to the invitation in unexpected ways. A friend of a friend who was not on the list commented that it was a terrible idea and inappropriate. Perhaps this person thought we were throwing a surprise party for Jim, which it was not. A couple friends who were invited declined because it was uncomfortable for them. Unfortunately, one person did not read the invitation carefully and called me to offer condolences and to apologize for not knowing Jim had died—which he had not. By and large, however, people were delighted to be asked and eager to have a few good moments with Jim. Roughly 100 attended.

In contrast to the week before, Jim was up early that day and almost like his former self. Hospice had put him on a short-term course of steroids to support him so he could truly enjoy the party. It was understood the treatment would only continue until side effects became troubling or until the disease outpaced the benefits of the drug. In that case, Jim would slowly taper off the medication. Today, however, he was energetically arranging the lawn furniture as I cautioned him to conserve his strength, but he felt great and would not listen. Preparation for the party was extensive and I was already an overwhelmed caregiver. Renee and my long-time friend from the San Francisco South Bay, Debbie, came to my rescue as I had fallen behind when guests began to arrive.

Shortly after greeting a number of guests, Jim took a seat under the pergola off to one side of the backyard. People would go to him in small groups to visit with him before making way for others to do so. We all marveled at how good Jim looked, despite his weight loss and advanced illness. A memory board of photographs composed by Renee decorated a food table. Roberta brought an elaborately decorated scrapbook with sections that illustrated Jim's interests. The invitations encouraged people to bring photos and to write down memories to go in the book. Jim thought it was unnecessary because "nobody would want to do that."

The afternoon was a powerful exchange of love and lessons. For many, it was the first time they understood Jim was receiving hospice care. I was so grateful Jo agreed to come to the party even though it was her day off. I was able to introduce her to people and they felt comfortable asking questions about hospice while enjoying their pie. I was also able to tell Jo of a special conversation between Jim and me the week before.

After Jo left from her weekly visit, Jim asked me if I liked her. "Yes, I really like her. She's very good at what she does and I appreciate that you have someone you can trust to help you through this time," I'd replied.

"Do you think you could become friends with her?" he asked.

"Sure, I admire her and think we would have some things in common," I responded.

"I want you to be friends with her."

"Hm," I thought. Jim was being very sweet, but I also knew this might be another way of taking care of me. Either way, it seemed like a good idea. At the party, I told Jo of the conversation and she was very touched because Jim had become a patient she enjoyed. She said she was honored that he wanted us to be friends.

The pie-eating party spilled into the front and backyards. Guests were invited to help themselves to as many slices of pie as they wanted. He may not have realized how beloved he was, but Jim did know the party and opportunity to see him in a relatively good state was a gift to those who gathered to fete him. He posed for pictures with large groups of friends and exchanged love with each of them.

For me, the main lesson of the day had more to do with Jim and his understanding of his own importance in the world. Following the party, Jim sat in his easy chair, still charged up from the energy and love but exhausted from the day of activity. I brought the album and notes people had written and he sat there reading them, weeping. Once composed, he said quietly, "I had no idea how many people *really* love me."

Still on the steroid prescription Jo monitored for him, we attended a marriage vow renewal of Jim's oldest daughter a few weeks later and enjoyed that celebration with family members, as well as a large number of Renee and Jay's friends. It was a day that made her father happy to know she was doing well. Renee and Roberta are both capable women and good mothers. Seeing them happy and doing well brought more peace to Jim than almost anything else.

Two moments stand out from that day for me. At one point in the backyard, Jim stopped me as we walked near the area where Renee and Jay had earlier said their vows. He told me he would marry me all over again. Later that day, when his energy level dipped, Jim sat on the sofa in Renee's family room. Before long, several of Renee's female friends were clustered around Jim, listening to his silly stories and laughing. The women may have flirted just a little but it was fun to watch because Jim had endearing qualities that many women found appealing, including a great sense of humor and a cache of jokes at the ready for any new audience. It just showed me how much it means to a terminal cancer patient to be treated like a normal person instead of someone to be pitied. I kept my eye on the scene because it gave me so much joy. It was a great day for both of us. It is those sweet moments and others during our nearly two-year odyssey that stand out as so joyful. They are moments I cling to, knowing Jim was fully engaged with his loved ones and me.

THE BIGGEST ADVENTURE

It was near the end of the Slice of Life party that word first came to me that Jim and I were planning a trip to Yellowstone National Park. Really? "OK," I thought, "that medicine they gave him today is making him talk crazy." While trying to appear nonchalant in response to the news, I was panicking inside thinking this cannot happen. How could I tell him "no?"

I spoke with Jo about it but was her response was unexpected. She was delighted at Jim's interest in such a venture. "No, no," I thought. "I can't pull something like this off." Truly, I had come to rely so heavily on hospice's support that I could not imagine being a thousand miles away and unable to get telephone advice on what to do if Jim's situation changed. Jim began talking enthusiastically of this trip and I became really scared.

Furthermore, he wanted to make the trip in a used car he had purchased from a friend some months before. He had been driving what we referred to as a "beater" car for work and golfing, but his friend wanted to sell this low-mileage more luxurious vehicle for a good price. Jim was intrigued, but hesitant to spend the money. I had urged him to treat himself for once, and he finally did. There had been a few minor things that required repair, but it was a nice ride and Jim really liked it. To this point in time we had only driven it to doctor's appointments and on short local trips. I was not terribly confident we would not become stranded on a long trip. I had a little SUV, but Jim liked the smoother ride of his car.

When Jo was scheduled for her next visit, I was rather hoping Jim would come to his senses and change his mind. While selfishly listening to the conversation and hoping for a "no go" on the trip, I had a change of heart. What changed for me was learning I had been under the false impression that Jim had already been to Yellowstone and wanted to return with me. It turned out that, like the horseback hunting trip he often had spoken of and never taken, Jim had never actually been to Yellowstone. During her visit, Jo described what hospice could do to prepare us. Before the meeting was over, I knew I had to make this happen and that it would be an important gift for Jim. Little did I know that it was a gift we would share in equally.

We decided to make the trip as soon as possible and were scheduled to be on our way within fifteen days of the party. We would have to go "off" hospice for the duration of our travels and then come back on as soon as we returned home. I attempted to anticipate potential trouble such as altitude and ordered oxygen tanks to bring with us. His meds were all working well and I was instructed on a couple of adjustments I could make should a couple possible "what ifs" occur. Jim had recently had his ascites drained, so we knew that would not be a problem. I purchased a new cell phone and managed to at least learn to make calls on it before we left town.

This trip also presented my best chance to tackle a necessary accommodation that Jim had resisted. Over the past two years, even before his diagnosis, Jim had occasionally experienced minor bladder incontinence, mostly at night. In recent weeks, the problem increased. It was something that was unpleasant for me because we shared a bed, but now we were going to travel and I didn't want to damage hotel property or have Jim be embarrassed. I once again, more firmly, approached the subject of adult incontinence protection, with emphasis on "protection."

"Jim, we are going to be sleeping in beds that belong to someone else. It is time to accept responsibility for making sure you don't damage them and also to protect yourself from embarrassment," I urged. He grudgingly agreed. I went shopping and tucked the package of disposable underwear in a large tote in the back of the car.

Rather than driving in two days, I planned two overnight stops in Reno and Boise that I thought would suit Jim's endurance for travel each day. We loved gambling in Reno and I could not see driving through without stopping, especially since our previous visit I initially thought would be our last stop in Reno together. I still don't understand why, but Jim was vehemently opposed to my making advance hotel reservations. It must have been a misunderstanding, but I finally went ahead and made reservations in Reno, insisting Reno would be very busy in August.

Plans were almost complete and Jim still insisted we take his car rather than my known-to-be-reliable Honda. I decided to just cross my fingers and hope for the best. I explained to Jim and our hospice team that if his condition worsened or if at any time I felt beyond my ability with respect to his care, that I would bundle Jim into the car and make a mad dash for home so he could return to hospice care. All agreed.

Normally Jim liked for me to drive, but on the morning we left for his big Yellowstone adventure, he got behind the wheel. Yes, he was on morphine, but it specifically targeted his pain and left him otherwise alert and functional. I regularly checked his energy level, which was good because he was still on the energy-enhancing medication he had been put on for the party. The benefits would eventually erode, but for now he was fairly strong.

We stopped at Dixon to see his parents' grave and to allow Jim to have a moment of contemplation. He again spoke to his parents and said he would see them soon. Jim had always claimed to be an atheist, but it was moments like this that made me think he was more agnostic. Perhaps it was just that he framed his understanding of death in the only way he had been nominally exposed to: a more-or-less Christian view of heaven. I didn't attempt to analyze it at the time, but this was clearly an important moment of acknowledgement to himself of his impending death.

We arrived in Reno surrounded by motorcycles so Jim conceded it was a good idea I had insisted on reservations. We checked in and rested up a bit before getting some food. Jim was in a good mood and seemed almost his old self, except that he was eating very little at that time. He had finally decided he could not drink alcohol and expect to have a good night. So we chose to eat at the coffee shop restaurants where we could get a salad or soup and less rich food choices. Otherwise, Jim went down to the poker tables and I went off to my machines, as usual. We made a point of getting to bed at a reasonable hour to arise refreshed for the next leg of the trip. That night, before bed, Jim emerged from the bathroom in his new underwear. He did a silly dance around the room and laughed with me to cope with his initial embarrassment. It was a positive breakthrough that required no further discussion. I was proud that he was brave enough to confront the matter so directly.

Once we arrived in West Yellowstone, I tried a couple lodging options unsuccessfully and Jim began to come unglued. He was sure we would not find a room and saw this as a major obstacle to enjoying a successful trip. There was no need to remind him he had inexplicably insisted I not make reservations, so I asked him to remain calm as I proceeded to find a solution.

At the third motel, a young clerk gave me a list of accommodations in the area and checked off some that she thought might have rooms available, indicating what her preference would be. I took the list and Jim did a fair amount of whining while I began making calls. It wasn't his illness that made him so distressed. We all have our flaws and Jim had always been what I call a "catastrophizer": someone who thinks every little bump in the road is a big issue. Within two or three calls, we found a motel room opening and drove there to look at the room. We took the room, which looked more suited to traveling college students, but now our adventure was back on track and Jim was comforted to be over that impediment.

It was just around noon so we decided to get a bite to eat and to take a drive into the park. So far, I was grateful the trip was going well. The car was operating like a dream and I was able to overcome any little issues. Before heading to the park, however, Jim wanted to find a fishing guide to take him fishing on the Madison River, a dream he'd had since he was a young man. We connected with a guide who was hoping to find a second person for a trip he had scheduled. That kept costs down for the customers and it was comforting to me that Jim would have two men with him.

Jim was not inclined to say anything to the guide about his condition as plans were being made, so I felt it was only fair to explain Jim's special needs to the guide. He needed to know what he was getting into just in case Jim had some sort of difficulty. No problem, so Jim and I next headed to purchase the licenses for the next day's fishing trip. Then we took off to drive into the park.

If you have never been to Yellowstone, the park is set up in two major loops that would take a couple hours each to drive, so we took the southern loop on this first afternoon. I had no idea how easy it would be to see wildlife and the amazing sites of the park from the car. It couldn't have been more perfect for our needs if I had ordered it constructed just for us.

No sooner had we driven through the park entry than we had a buffalo walking alongside cars on the road. The park's beautiful expanses were awe-inspiring at every turn. However, Jim had some difficulty breathing as we topped the Continental Divide. He refused oxygen and was fine as soon as we dropped to a comfortable elevation. When we stopped the car at the Paint Pots, Jim took one look at the boardwalk between the different viewing stations and stayed in the car. After half a day of driving and getting his fishing trip set up, he was out of energy for walking. I quickly made my tour and took pictures to show him when I returned to the car. The rest of the drive was perfect and we headed back to the motel at dinner time to rest up and decide what to have for dinner.

There was a small restaurant across the road from our motel. The simple meal was good, then we headed back to the motel. Jim was very tired and needed to be helped up the small incline. He was shocked to be so out of breath, but I reminded him that altitude was also a factor here. He refused oxygen when I offered it. We slept and got up early on Day Two in Yellowstone to meet his fishing guide.

The young guide was very helpful answering our questions. We met the other fisherman who would be with him, an older man who was very pleasant. I was worried if Jim would be safe, but I felt optimistic knowing that he would be sitting in a boat and that he tended to rise up to overcome challenges when something engaged his interest fully.

I left them and spent the day exploring West Yellowstone, awaiting a call to pick Jim up.

Late that afternoon when I went to pick him up, Jim was doing his best to keep up appearances but it was clear to me he was exhausted beyond words. At the same time, he was elated at the experience. That was when I learned, despite explaining his trip to the men who sold licenses, Jim had purchased the wrong licenses. The guide and other customer had to turn around and come back to purchase the correct licenses for Jim before they could put a line in the river. I thanked him profusely for not abandoning Jim in this matter. Jim had been humiliated, but he was grateful for the kindness shown to him. The guide was very gracious and promised to e-mail pictures he had taken. The three men shook hands and parted ways before I helped Jim into the car. He could hardly wait to tell me the guide said that of the sixty or more guided trips he had led that summer, Jim had caught the biggest trout. To this day, a picture of Jim holding that fish makes me smile when I pass it.

His voice was weak and he was cold, but Jim was glowing with happiness and a sense of achievement. He slept before I left to bring food back to the room. He had been too focused on fishing to eat any snacks during the day. I picked up soup and sandwiches at a little café and returned to the room. Jim was hungry, but did not get up. His head was propped up in the bed. When I set up the little table for us to eat, he asked if I would feed him in bed. I brought the cup of soup over.

"I mean, can you *feed* me?" he asked.

My throat tightened and my eyes stung. I wanted to cry that my husband was so weak and helpless in this moment. I made an excuse about needing another napkin from the table so I could look away and check the expression on my face. I did not want Jim to see the pain I felt. When I turned back to Jim, I was hurting but composed. I carefully spooned the soup for him. He ate about half of the portion and a couple bites of sandwich before saying he wanted to sleep. I excused myself after eating my meal and wept in the bathroom while getting myself ready for bed.

Day Three in Yellowstone would be a trip around the northern loop of the park before heading back to Boise. Jim seemed OK with me driving and we found this loop of the park was most eventful. We were stopped on the road by a large herd of buffalo. We stopped at Old Faithful. It was a struggle, but Jim managed to walk with help from the car to the outside viewing area for the geyser. Conveniently, it blasted off within a minute of our arrival so no time was wasted. Then we drove through the area where the rangers stay and had a close-up experience with a herd of elk, bulls with enormous antler racks and large harems.

Amazing photos in hand from the trip, we headed for home, chattering endlessly about all we had seen and experienced. I felt so blessed that Jim had finally had this watershed experience he had thought about most of his life. I was grateful to the greater powers that things had gone so well. If the car broke down on the way home, it would an inconvenience, but not a crisis. We had already accomplished the goal of Jim's dream adventure. The good luck continued all the way home. I enjoyed still another evening of gambling in Reno, but Jim preferred, and surely needed, to rest.

We arrived home without incident and I immediately called hospice to reactivate the relationship. The hospice professionals were happy to hear about our successful trip and seemed to revel with Jim as he described all he had seen and done. We enjoyed looking at our photographs and were delighted with the ones the guide emailed to me. From those we selected a couple to frame for Jim's den, which I was preparing for the time it would be converted to his full-time end-of-life space.

It was around this time that, while marveling about the wonderful people who had come into our lives and the amazing support of hospice, Jim suggested I write a book about our experiences. He also, once again, thanked me for my caregiving support. I, of course, could not imagine doing anything else. But I initially thought Jim's suggestion about the book was just one of those things people say and never act on. When it came up again, he made it clear he was serious because he felt telling our story could be helpful to others. I promised him I would write our story.

CHAPTER SUMMARY

- For patients whose death process is slow, there is opportunity to deal with the pain of many types of losses. Job, pets, hobbies, and treasured possessions are among the losses a terminal patient may grieve over. Difficult as it is to observe, this is an important part of one's preparation to die.

- Don't hesitate to use good times to create memories with loved ones while the patient remains interested in doing so. Even though it may test the endurance of the patient, facilitate their wishes to enjoy family and friends in special settings. Taking a long-dreamed-of trip can be a gift to the patient, the family, and to the caregiver.

- Stopping treatment is a very personal decision and may be well-supported by a palliative care team. It can be alarming to loved ones, but it is best to listen to the dying loved one's feelings, needs, and end-of-life goals to better understand their choices. Stopping treatment is the patient's choice when they can speak for themselves.

- During the course of a lengthy disease, there will become a time when bad days begin to outnumber good days. Prepare mentally for this time as it is most likely calling hospice will bring relief and needed support to make the most of the patient's remaining time and to support the caregiver.

- Even the most well-meaning and correct advice from a spouse is sometimes not well received. Oftentimes the patient "gets it" after testing their boundaries or when the same information is delivered by a professional. It is important that the spouse caregiver not take this personally. Whenever possible, ask a medical person to weigh in on the topic. When the loved one is better at accepting undesired or unpleasant information from someone other than the spouse, the important thing is that the information is communicated, not who delivers it.

- As explained by our hospice team, some patients are good at hiding their depression and intentions to abbreviate their lives. Listen to their advice. In the case of a slow decline toward a natural death, it is important to assure the loved one about the things known to matter to them. Let them know the matters that concern them will be in good hands going forward.

- As sad as final visits with beloved friends can be, saying goodbye to treasured possessions that are associated with wonderful memories can also be very painful for the dying. The patient needs to grieve each loss and not made to feel their sadness over "things" is unimportant.

- Pre-death gatherings and celebrations are increasingly popular and can go a long way in helping everyone settle their feelings around an impending loss. It is a wonderful time to be open about love and to share with the dying individual how they have made life better for others.

- If the resources are available, it is important to support important goals of the dying. These may involve the patient's long-time interests, their beliefs, or their connection with others. For example, an outdoorsman who communed with nature on a regular basis throughout life, it is natural he would want to do so near his end of life.

Resources

www.cancer.org/treatment/survivorship-during-and-after-treatment/staying-active/nutrition/nutrition-during-treatment.html

Chapter Five

CAREGIVING, DIAGNOSIS TO DEATH

"It is a loving wish to die before the one we entirely love,
but a selfish wish to die before the one who entirely loves us.
It is one of the most painful parts of our condition that,
if we are fortunate enough to have a true friend,
one or the other of these things must happen, unless,
indeed by a rare chance (as by shipwreck)
both die suddenly, unexpectedly and together."
– From the diary of John Stuart Mill, English philosopher, 1854
Vulnerability and Loss of Autonomy

A woman I once met while taking a course on caregiving for older adults told me a personal story about her own caregiving experience. We were roughly the same age and she had experienced a serious hospitalization at one point that required a lengthy recuperation period. Once her health had been stabilized, she was sent home with twenty-four-hour caregiving provided by a home care agency. She lived alone and was terrified.

As challenging as it had been to accept personal care assistance in the hospital, now she would be home alone with strange caregivers. Not only was she totally dependent on a new set of caregivers for care, she would be in a bind if they did not show up on time. She also realized how vulnerable she was as she had not had time to secure important belongings and personal paperwork. Every day was a challenge to allow those strangers to deliver personal care services and to trust they would not take advantage of her. I have never forgotten her story of vulnerability and how that shaped her empathy for older adults.

This sense of loss of autonomy and the accompanying vulnerability is what confronts older adults who must have help and individuals facing a slow, natural death. We often hear how "stubborn" they are in refusing to accept help, but it is important to keep in mind the simultaneous fear and loss of autonomy they must confront to accept help in ways nobody wants to need. Helping them overcome their fears requires patience, timing, and compassion on the part of the caregiver.

Additionally, as the patient moves toward death and begins to experience the expected physical changes, such as incontinence, there is shame and embarrassment at requiring a type of help mostly thought of as for children. Late-life incontinence is related to advanced age and declining health. Dealing with incontinence can be as difficult for the caregiver as for the care recipient. That is why these subjects should be discussed long before the matter becomes reality. Agreements to work together and without judgment of one another can go a long way in smoothing the process. In time, the dying move beyond caring about the physical realm to focus on transitioning as they sleep more and more. When a lack of concern on the part of the dying individual ensues, it can relieve some of the stress from providing personal care.

Some older adults begin to receive care such as assistance with walking, transportation, and household chores long before there is sickness or a terminal diagnosis. In these cases, companionship is often an important part of the caregiver role. However, caring for a terminal patient requires an extensive skillset and specific understanding of the process and the wishes of the patient and family. When a caregiver whose initial role was to help maintain the home, cook, and drive to appointments can continue after a patient receives a terminal diagnosis, the care recipient may be more amenable to accepting increased help.

CAREGIVER SELF-CARE

For a caregiver at any stage, knowing when to ask for help of any kind is crucial. I am sharing with you my story because it is important for readers to understand that I don't come from a place of all-knowing and super-human qualities that enabled me to sail through this challenging period of my life. Unfortunately, the response from my body to the bad news of my husband's diagnosis had the potential to render me useless right from the start. It was not the thought of caregiving that shook me, but grief and my overwhelming concern for Jim. My reaction was an intense subconscious and physical stress response to our life-altering circumstances.

When I had just learned of his diagnosis, it was too soon to be overwhelmed with caregiving responsibilities as Jim was still active and able to physically care for himself. This was the time when my role was that of a loving, supportive spouse who provides a calm and safe emotional respite to the loved one coping with the new realization of terminal illness. However, I was so devastated by his diagnosis and what was ahead for him that I became ill. Though vital that I consciously accept the truth of my husband's diagnosis, once the diagnosis was confirmed I could not sleep and I had a serious, unrelenting case of acid reflux for the first time in my life. A few days into this, I was so depleted I could not drive my car. I was not thinking clearly and had trouble communicating sensibly. I knew it was time for me to see a doctor.

Caring for my husband did weigh heavily on me and did exact a toll, but I was able to manage it with help from my physician. It also helped that I am a positive person and attuned to gratitude and seeking lessons of love as I go through life. Seeking help when I needed it helped me focus my energy on Jim's needs. I needed to be in good shape for that, so I worked at my physical and emotional health throughout the two years he remained with me and beyond. It is absolutely true that the caregiver needs to take care, too. It is equally true that one needs to use the resources of friends and professionals to help during challenging times or when strength has waned.

Do not hesitate to ask for the help you need. Those who care about you want to help and want your guidance as to how they can help. Give it to them so they can support you.

HOSPICE PATIENT NEEDS

For anyone new to caregiving, I have compiled a list of tasks which will ultimately be needed by the hospice patient. Before hiring a caregiver, look for training in the following areas.

CLIENT PERSONAL CARE

Assist with dressing

Toileting assistance with commode, toilet, or briefs for bed-bound status

If catheter present, empty bag

If ostomy present, empty bag

Hair care, including shampoo

Brush teeth twice daily or clean dentures daily (oral care if patient is comatose and/or not eating/drinking)

Shaving daily

Nail care, trimming, and cleaning and filing as needed

Bathing assistance, including sponge bath in bed. Apply emollient lotions.

Assist family in medication administration, including recordkeeping for doses given/missed and reorders

Recording daily events including meals, intake and output

Provide supportive attention: listening, reading, playing music or programs, and prayer if desired

Call hospice with observed changes and instructions for interventions

If patient is on infection precautions, know how to follow the specific precautions

Maintain quiet demeanor and surroundings; refrain from pressuring unwilling patient about eating or drinking

MEAL MANAGEMENT

Prepare appropriate meals and supplements. Adapt texture (chop or puree) as needed

Feed, if necessary. Understand dysphagia (choking) precautions if warranted

Offer fluids; follow dysphagia precautions as needed

MOTILITY

Assist with walking and using mobility devices (cane, walker, wheelchair)

Understand ergonomically correct transfers from bed to chair and use of gait belt and Hoyer lift, if appropriate

Employ correct bed techniques of turning patient and changing briefs and linens for bedfast clients

HOME MANAGEMENT

Keep kitchen and dishes clean

Wash clothing and change linens

Manage oxygen and respiratory equipment if used; routine hygienic care of devices

Frequently dispose of trash, at least twice daily

Vacuum/sweep/dust home as needed

Keep bathroom and bedside commode hygienic

YOUR FIRST DAY AS A CAREGIVER

Caregiving begins from the first moment you are told by a physician that your loved one is seriously ill or when a terminal diagnosis is made. As you absorb the knowledge of your loved one's diagnosis, your first caregiving role is to provide calm and comfort. This includes beginning to find your role and assert yourself as a health care advocate. Several cancer patients have told me they could not hear a word the doctor said after the word "cancer" was first uttered. I'm sure the same is true for any life-altering diagnosis. As caregiver, you must pay attention to the details your loved one is too overwhelmed to take in. Your initial list of tasks will be something like this:

- Listening, note-taking, and asking questions about the diagnosis and care instructions.
- Keeping track of an appointment calendar.
- Noting changes in diet and activities to report to the physician.
- Understanding and administering new medication regimens.
- Supporting your loved one in decisions.
- Non-judgmental listening.
- Driving to medical appointments.
- Listening.
- Listening.
- Reassuring.
- Listening some more.

My best and most basic advice for new caregivers throughout the time a loved one relies on them for care and support is:

Be prepared. Be informed and anticipate next steps to help manage stress.

Be flexible. Things can change suddenly that alter your entire routine.

Know your limits. Anticipate your own needs before you are overwhelmed or sick.

PATIENT RECEPTIVITY

Even as a loving spouse providing care, there were certain things my husband would not accept from me. In years past, he had rebuffed my advice about handling minor aches and pains with remarks such as, "Where did you get your medical degree?"

Now, in this tender time of caregiving for his terminal illness, the last thing I wanted was to have Jim rebuff good information because it came from me. I quickly learned to find ways for the doctor or another professional to deliver it. Always present during appointments where new information was expected, I could direct pointed questions to the doctor. Even if he forgot, I could repeat to Jim the information preceded by "I recall the doctor said . . . "

Rather than waste energy on feeling hurt that my spouse didn't see me as an all-knowing resource, I decided to use the resources around us as they were intended. On occasion, I got a dirty look from Jim if I brought up something we had already disagreed over, but at least I got the information to him from a professional, and it was worth dealing with his momentary disapproval to have that course correction.

Someone once asked me if it made me angry or hurt when Jim accepted information from Jo that he could not hear from me. "No," I responded. "I don't care how he gets what he needs as long as he does get it, and I appreciate that he trusts professionals like Jo."

APPROPRIATE CAREGIVING HELP

Even when needed, having caregivers in the home is helpful in some ways but intrusive in ways that quickly become apparent. They need to be shown what to do and how, and you need to prepare them to relate to your family member. Some communities have options, but if you don't have the monetary wherewithal to hire paid caregivers, friends and family members may be your only resource. Especially when a patient is approaching or in active stages of dying, caregivers must have a calm, quiet, and gentle manner. Loud talking or laughing, over-stimulation, expecting a patient to "perk up" and respond to things previously enjoyed (sunshine, upbeat music, etc.) is inappropriate. Work is performed gently, quietly, with utmost respect, and at the pace the patient can endure.

In the case of my husband, I was able to handle all the caregiving responsibility until he was no longer able to walk. Though he had lost a lot of weight, he was still too heavy for me to pick up in the event of a fall, and I was inexperienced at some of the procedures for hygiene. When I first needed help with Jim, I didn't know what to look for. Below are some of the most important things to look for in a caregiver, some I learned from my friend and experienced caregiver Dini, and others I learned "on the job."

The right person. My first paid caregiver came from an agency. This woman's limited English made it difficult for me to explain Jim's needs. She moved so quickly that she made Jim, who was now slow and weak, very nervous. She was motivated and wanted to clean the bathroom at one point, so I gave her the tools and products, but she did not understand that the toilet brush was just for toilets. I had to re-sanitize all the surfaces she inappropriately "cleaned" with it. She also did not understand that the rubber gloves she wore to work with Jim were not to be saved and reused the next day. All of this suggested a lack of training.

Despite a visit from the agency supervisor before she was placed, this person was not a match, so I requested a replacement. I later learned the woman had worked in a skilled nursing facility and was accustomed to handling several patients in a production-type situation; dress, wheel to breakfast, change the bed, et cetera, in rapid succession. She may have been a good worker in that environment with people who were somewhat stronger and better able to communicate than Jim, but her fast-pace work methods were all wrong for an advanced hospice patient.

Security. It may sound negative, but when you hire care workers, it is important that you take precautions. Remove valuables and personal items that are meaningful because if they are misplaced or lost, it can be unfair to the caregiver or to you. Be sure the agency has bonded their workers and get this information in writing.

Medications. Secure all medications because your hospice patient will have a supply of prescriptions that are coveted by those with prescription drug addictions. I do not recommend delegating dispensing of medications to anyone other than yourself or a trusted immediate family member or hospice worker. Dosages administered need to be recorded so you can keep the patient comfortable and stable.

Food. Initially, Jim wanted to continue eating his favorite foods and large meals. He was a meat-and-potatoes guy. However, this became problematic as his disease progressed. Rich and heavy foods could not be held down so we experimented with foods that were easy on his system and comforting. As his disease began to take up more space in his abdomen, eating became a far less satisfying experience. His eating changes and loss of appetite were gradual and I did my best to adjust to each change. Eventually, he lost interest in food, but in the early stages, we did our best to give him smaller, easy-to-digest meals without much restriction as to his preferences. Ultimately, in the late stages he was no longer eating, and caregivers need to understand this is normal.

Hospice special needs. If you hire from outside, make sure the agency and worker understand what hospice is and where your loved one is in the process of dying. If they have never worked with someone who is actively dying, it may seem cruel to them not to feed a patient who has stopped eating. I found one worker trying to feed Jim cereal when he had not eaten for several days. It was awkward to explain to her (away from his hearing) that he had expressed he was ready to leave and more nourishment could complicate his process. Jim was still sipping water and having occasional frozen pops, but I found that everyone wanted to feed him endless popsicles when they visited. It was just too hard for most outsiders to imagine that not eating was a normal and painless way for him to allow his body to slowly shut down.

I could see Jim's skin color was changing and that he did not have much time. Like the feeding issue, it was unsettling to both Jim and me when there was too much noise and commotion in the house or if visitors stayed too long. Again, hospice was helpful in providing an expert explanation to others as to Jim's needs. I confess to feeling a bit disappointed that there was little time for me to sit and hold his hand and be alone with him, as I had hoped having help would give me the chance to do this. When everyone left, Jim was tired and needed to be left alone to sleep.

CARE AND HELP ALTERNATIVES

Finally, if you are reading this book in mid-life and are not in immediate need of making care arrangements, you have no idea at what age your family member might need hospice care or what the best options for care will be at that time. Had Jim and I been older, it is very likely I would have had to consider placing him in a hospice health care setting where I could visit daily. This requires substantial financial resources but is an especially important option for couples who have no family members who can step in to help or when family members are not the best choice for care.

If caring for your loved one at home, be prepared for well-meaning volunteers whose help may not actually materialize when you need it. Rather than be impatient and expect that someone should *want* to help you, take this advice in now: if you need help, be specific with each individual about what you need and when. There will be times that people do not come through for you or when the help they offer really isn't helpful. But others will come through in surprising ways when you most need them because they are better suited to support you. Better to be pleasantly surprised when the help comes through than to waste energy on wishing someone else would do something that doesn't come easily to them.

Before the need arises for your loved one, I would encourage you to spend time looking into what options and resources are available for caregiving in your community. Special hospital wings, residential care homes, and other facilities may offer hospice care in your area if in-home hospice care is not available.

BE FLEXIBLE

From the first day of Jim's diagnosis, my lesson seemed to be that I cannot control everything. Being prepared is usually about having specific plans in place, but what about when you don't control the course of events? In the event of terminal illness, being prepared means bracing yourself to hang on for the ride and being emotionally ready (as much as is possible) for any of the many options and decisions that come your way. The best way to say it is this: emotionally prepare yourself to accept that which cannot be planned by talking about the (known) possibilities and options in advance.

Jim was in charge of his decisions about his medical care, even if I was uncomfortable at times. He would make spontaneous decisions for which I would need to adjust my plans or my thinking. Early in his process we would sometimes learn new information that would suddenly shift the trajectory of his situation and cause a mental rewrite of the activities to support new goals. The possibility of a treatment option could put us on a plane to visit specialists in another city. One minute he would decide to stop a treatment and the next minute I was booking a family horseback ride. These times were especially hard, but "let go" was my new mantra. The Greater Power was in charge and my job was to serve as my best self, helping Jim navigate his way home.

KNOW YOUR LIMITS

Caregivers need to remember that being an effective caregiver does not require that you become debilitated by your efforts. You won't have much time to think about it until after your loved one has transitioned, but you will have a life to live afterward. Whether your new life will involve continuing to parent, enjoying a career, or starting something new in your new life, plan to stay healthy so you can live your new life fully. That is what those who love you, including the departed, want for you.

Whether it is about getting enough sleep or respite breaks from caregiving or keeping in mind physical abilities that are limited by age, it is crucial to be realistic about what you can and cannot do. You might get lucky lifting your loved one once or twice, but tweaking your back can put you out of commission and create much bigger problems. Stress and being tired will make you more vulnerable to injury. That is why you must plan to have help even before you feel it is a full-time need. Ask yourself the following:

- How many nights can I go without sleep and still be effective?
- Can I lift an inert person back into bed and know I won't hurt myself?
- Am I emotionally strong enough to redirect or comfort my loved one who wants something unrealistic (unsafe transfer of someone who cannot bear weight, something

to eat when they cannot swallow, a deliberate overdose of medicine)?

Be wise about all of the above even before hospice is on board, but know that you will have immediate back up and support in these and other challenging matters as soon as hospice enters the picture. From that point forward, any time you don't know what to do, hospice is a phone call away, twenty-four seven.

Jo speaks of giving personal hygiene care to a patient in another section of this chapter, and I would say this is a matter for which many adults know they have limited caregiving ability. I admit that I could never have given Jim a bed bath because of my limited strength and lack of expertise, but it was changing my husband's adult incontinence garment that truly intimidated me. I was able to change him at night when nobody was around. I did not want him to feel judged or that I was offended, so I made myself be able to assist, but it was a challenge.

If you have not tested your limits before, I would suggest that you listen to the hospice experts. They have worked with hundreds, if not thousands, of clients and their families. They are aware that many people cannot handle some aspects of caregiving. Caregiving is a loving and selfless act, but it is best to keep a few paces back from the outer limits of your abilities by erring on the side of caution.

Being smart about your own health is vital to providing the loving support you want to give to your loved one as they transition from this life. It will also help protect your health for the life you still have to live.

CAREGIVING FROM A HOSPICE PERSPECTIVE

Hiring a caregiver is surprisingly expensive. The availability of workers to fill the growing need in America for this type of help is already in crisis mode. The imbalance between need and funding will only grow larger as greater numbers of aged adults need help. Insufficient numbers of older adults are prepared to fund the actual cost of in-home caregiving, which normally exceeds eighteen dollars an hour in 2017. Therefore, planning one's end of life must include financial planning for the expenses to cover the final needs.

Furthermore, if your need is not immediate and you are truly looking into plans for your future, an agreement with your niece (or son or grandchild) for help when you are frail or in hospice mode may not be suitable or sufficient in ten or twenty years. Your niece may have moved out of the area or have changes in her own family needs that make her ineligible or unavailable to assist you when the time comes. It is a fine plan for now to list her as your caregiver because we never know when we will need the help. However, you need to revisit your plans annually to make sure they remain viable and to update them as needed. That said, here are my recommendations:

Dying is normally a slow, incremental process. Therefore, one should decide who will provide care when the time comes to make preparations such as creating end-of-life planning documents. This should also include where one will want to spend one's last days. As I describe a variety of settings in which a hospice client can receive care, it is important to note that some options are not available in every community. Likewise, when a hired caregiver in the home becomes necessary, as described below, many communities have limited resources for locating staff familiar with end-of-life care. I would encourage all readers to seek out and familiarize themselves with the hospice settings and caregiving staffing options in their area long before they are needed. Some assisted living facilities can also provide added hospice care, as required.

Other settings will have more limited capacity and will require the family to participate or hire specialized help to supplement what is normally offered. In some cases, the facility has connections with qualified individuals they can put their residents in touch with for private hire.

As awareness of end-of-life care and hospice grows, many communities are expanding their services to accommodate the growing number of individuals choosing to die at home. If this interests you, you may wish to volunteer now to support your community in developing further hospice options. Your local senior center, council on aging, hospitals, and government agencies that serve the elderly may have information and volunteer opportunities to grow their programs.

For those living in senior facilities or communities, it is important to know the policies of your place of residence to know whether end-of-life care is provided or not. Life care communities located in California offer three levels of care (independent, residential, and skilled nursing). They generally require a resident living in the independent portion of their facility to be responsible for hiring and compensating outside caregiver assistance. They may require a resident to locate to the skilled nursing facility when on hospice. Policies for supplemental outside care will vary between facilities at the independent, residential, and skilled nursing levels of care, as well as from state to state.

Some facilities also offer assisted living within the resident's apartment as opposed to independent living, providing trained caregivers to give attention and assistance with medication management, bathing, dressing, and meals twenty-four hours a day. In this instance, staff will also coordinate services with a local hospice team and monitor residents to ensure they are comfortable. Commonly, family will provide long visits to supplement the care already provided.

Large elder care facilities often contain a skilled nursing unit, otherwise known as a nursing home, with twenty-four-hour nursing and aid avail-

ability. No hired caregiver is necessary here, and this is the only part of a senior facility where Medicaid health insurance would cover the cost of the stay for indigent or disabled Medicaid-eligible clients only. Medicare does fund hospice care at home and at any elder care facility or skilled nursing facility. In other words, a patient of financial means can privately pay for room and board while Medicare covers the additional hospice care. For those with private, long-term health care insurance, it is advisable to understand what portion of room and board and private caregiver costs will be covered.

Hospice provides episodic visits to the client and does not cover twenty-four-hour caretakers, so a client in any setting must have a personal caretaker, family member, or hired help by the time they require help with activities of daily living and personal care. If a spousal partner is unavailable or incapacitated, an alternate agent can hire help privately or through an agency.

Many spouses who are physically and emotionally capable still choose to supplement care with a hired person, letting go of the role of physical caretaking to focus on their role as spouse. Unfortunately, many spouses who are themselves frail are often left with the heavy caregiving responsibility. If family or friends cannot help and financial deficits prohibit hiring a caregiver, a person who qualifies for Medicaid may be able to find a Medicaid-funded caregiver for a portion of the twenty-four-hour period. Medicaid does not fund around-the-clock caretakers. Some hospice organizations may have limited access to charitable short-term funding to assist indigent clients in hiring caregivers. As mentioned in an earlier chapter, hospice can offer a one-time week of respite for the caregiver by placing the patient in a hospital and that is covered by Medicare.

If one is considering hiring a hospice caregiver, finding the right fit involves qualities quite different from those in finding a companion/caregiver for an elder in other circumstances. Look for a quiet, calm individual who is qualified by training and/or experience so they are confident and comfortable *with end-of-life care. Even the interview needs to be different from hiring another type of caregiver. Of course, they need to have cleared a criminal background check. And when all needs must focus on the desires of the dying, it is most important that these caregivers understand their own concerns and ideas must be set aside. I suggest you interview several caregivers and be direct with regard to the following:*

Religion. *If, for instance, the hospice patient has specific religious or atheistic beliefs, the caregiver must respect those. They should be comfortable hearing what the patient has to say and not offer them negative feedback about their beliefs nor proselytize.*

Medications. *A caregiver who is alarmed by the medications taken by hospice patients may not be appropriate. The family caregiver should not delegate control of the medication to a hired caregiver. The medications may be numerous and not of a nature used in everyday health care but they are for purposes of comfort and easing anxiety for someone who is transitioning out of this world. The most commonly misunderstood medication for people unfamiliar with its medical benefits is morphine (or its equivalent), which is used for both pain relief and shortness of breath. It is the treatment of choice for hospice patients in respiratory distress. Hospice staff will advise and teach the family caregiver how to administer morphine and other comfort medications for the benefit of the patient.*

Physical ability. *Check for physical strength, ability to turn someone independently in bed, or transfer ergonomically from a chair. There are specific procedures which minimize risk to caregiver and patient. Individuals providing this type of care should know these methods. Hospice can also provide this education to family members.*

Availability. *Once in the throes of active dying, a patient must be monitored and cared for twenty-four hours a day. Even if a spouse is the primary caregiver, they should rely on hired help so they can sleep. If a hired caregiver is unreliable, it is extremely stressful for the family caregiver and hospice client. You can consider hiring one person for twenty-four-hour coverage, or you may prefer three eight-hour helpers, though it isn't always necessary to have constant help if the spouse or family caregiver can manage alone part of the time. Check the resources in your community from the senior center or private nursing agencies. Locate them and speak to them, gathering information about their costs, etc. The Internet provides wider ranges of resources.*

Cultural differences. *When hiring someone to provide personal care you naturally screen the potential employee(s) to find a match for your values, personality, and the skills compatible with your needs. Spiritual beliefs support and guide the work of many caregivers and often aid them in handling ethical dilemmas they may encounter. A personal care worker's spiritual beliefs can also help them manage the stress of caregiving.*

The job of hired caregiver in this country is one that is currently filled by persons from many different cultures and belief systems. All caregivers seeking work with a dying patient should be screened for their familiarity with the processes that aid a comfortable death. Some caregivers may be unable to support the patient's wish to stop eating and drinking when they are ready to die, believing that choice may be forbidden by the caregiver's belief system. Based on their belief that a person should do everything in their power to keep a loved one alive, some caregivers may believe in calling 911 despite the patient's wish to die naturally.

Go below the surface in your interview to inquire about how prospective caregivers may approach future ethical dilemmas regarding resuscitation, aid in dying, family discord, feeding issues, and other potential difficult decision points. In my experience, the best caregivers are calm and compassionate, flexible, experienced in ergonomic transfers and in-bed care, efficient with strong work ethic, and ultimately guided by a higher force than their egos.

CHAPTER SUMMARY

- Whether a loved one is learning to accept assistance with transfers or is concerned about their personal possessions being safe, keep in mind that accepting help requires development of a level of trust and probably some practice. It is also important that care is given without making the patient feel judged.
- Self-care for the caregiver is critical. Brief times away from caregiving and time for a massage or visit with a friend can be renewing and restorative. If stress or lack of sleep become an issue, immediately seek medical attention so your ability to provide care is not compromised.
- The list of tasks caregivers must perform is lengthy, some of which family members may not feel comfortable with. The list is worthy of a discussion with the loved one to help decide what types of hired help may be needed.
- Preparation, flexibility, and knowing one's limits are central to successful caregiving. Anticipating next steps is a good skill but even more importantly, a caregiver should know there will be times when the direction changes or an unexpected occurrence needs to be addressed. Knowing when you need help, how to access it quickly, and what you cannot do is vitally important in order to be available to your loved one and to avoid burnout.
- Volunteer or hired help must be willing to support the patient as needed. In addition to addressing physical needs

effectively, appropriate help respects the spiritual/religious/ non-religious beliefs and culture of the patient. Further, there needs to be an understanding and willingness to respect the medication regimen and feeding or non-feeding status of the dying patient.

- If providing hospice care at home is not feasible or practical, most states have options where the hospice patient can receive care in another setting, such as a board-and-care home or a hospice facility.

Resources

**www.hospicefoundation.org/Hospice-Care/Caregiving **
Hospice Foundation of America offers a free downloadable copy of Caregiver's Guide to the Dying Process, available via Google.

www.nhpco.org
The National Hospice and Palliative Care Organization website has a "Learn About" section in which the CaringInfo page contains links to caregiving support.

www.momentsoflife.org
Video presentations of real-life hospice patients demystify hospice care

www.ec-online.net
Website for Alzheimer's disease and caregiving
resources including forums and newsletters

www.eldercare.gov
Federal government website connecting visitor to local elder
care services including county basic services such as respite for
caregivers, adult day programs, home delivered meals, and more.

www.caregiveraction.org
Website created to educate, support, and empower
those caring for chronically ill loved ones.

www.growthhouse.org
Website providing education on end-of-life care,
including disease education for caretakers

Chapter Six

DEATH DELIVERED COMFORT, PEACE AND HEALING

"The call of death is a call of love.
Death can be sweet if we answer it in the affirmative,
if we accept it as one of the great eternal forms
of life and transformation."
- Hermann Hesse, German novelist, 1950

THE DISTRACTION OF FEAR

Often there are distractions resulting from long-held beliefs or fears that stand between the patient and achieving a sense of peace at the end of their days. One elderly hospice patient of mine would not take the medications that would reduce her pain because of beliefs and fears about medicines and possible side effects. She suffered in pain week after week despite repeated explanations we were starting with low dosages and proceeding slowly in a safe and conservative manner. One day, my colleagues and I were surprised when she apologized, telling me she realized I meant no harm to her. She acknowledged her mistaken beliefs and asked to take the medicines she had not been willing to take. Upon using the medications prescribed, her complaints of pain became rare.

Near the end, some terminal patients find living more daunting than death. When the spouse of another patient told me what an extraordinarily active, vibrant go-getter she had been in her work and personal life, I realized being debilitated had to be especially difficult for her. The patient told me she was so tired of her cancer, being exhausted and limited in what she could accomplish, that she wanted to die quickly. At that time, only death by dehydration was legally permitted for accelerating the dying. As her doctor and our team would never intentionally advise using a medicine that would actually speed up the process, I mentioned to her the one method I had witnessed that would allow her to die within two weeks.

Her posture changed, showing rapt attention. Before I told her how it worked, I advised her to include her family in the decision-making process, so she asked her family to join us in the room. I slowly related to all gathered the details of not eating nor drinking, going into a slumber by the end of the first week, and dying in one's sleep within the second week. She quickly announced she wanted to start right away. I counseled her to wait at least a day to allow her family to process the information and their feelings about it, as well as for her to give the matter more thought. She agreed and resolutely called the next day to tell me she was beginning that day. Her family was bravely and tearfully supporting her. And she proceeded fearlessly forward, without pausing, to leave us eleven days later. Once she heard the truth of the means of a foreshortened illness, she wholeheartedly embraced it. By supporting her, the family was grateful she found a way to leave earth on her own terms.

Loved ones struggle to develop a level of comfort as their family member approaches death. One daughter of a hospice patient found the idea of allowing someone to stop eating horrifying at first. However, as she sat with the idea it gave her unexpected peace that the end would come sooner and her loved one would be spared unnecessary suffering. And it was still a natural death. I've seen lives come to a peaceful conclusion in three to eleven days after intake of nourishment and water stops.

ACTIVE DYING APPROACHES

By late September 2013, Jim was weak and napping often. He did not want to stay in bed full-time but required considerable help to his chair. He no longer dared step out the front door for fear his legs would give way even if I helped him step down from the threshold. I began playing New Age music at low volume in his room or when he was in the front room and preferring to sleep rather than watch television. Soon, he was asking me to put it on because he could not keep up with the people on the television.

Jim was eating little other than nutritional drinks from a can. We began using a walker with a seat to help him get to the bathroom. He insisted on standing at the toilet and on having privacy, until he lost his balance and fell into the bathtub one day. Fortunately, I always stood outside the door and the shower curtain rod held in place so the curtain helped break his fall and he was not injured. The near-miss convinced him to cooperate more agreeably with safety considerations I suggested.

Around this same time, I insisted on bringing a hospital bed into his den. Jim protested because he felt he was being kicked out of our bed, but I did not let up because I knew sleep was critical to both of us. Jo shared with me that she calls rented hospital beds "electric beds" —a term that seems to be less upsetting to her patients.

She explains to them that the bed gives them options for positions that are more comfortable. Jim complained for several days, saying the air mattress designed to protect him from pressure sores was uncomfortable. He let up when I purchased an egg-crate cushion in lieu of the air cushion. True, it overrode the benefits of the air mattress, but he was losing ground quickly. He was still moving about the house to some degree, so pressure sores were not yet a concern. Over time, since he had a television in his den/bedroom, Jim began enjoying more time in his den away from household activity and visitors. In addition to television, he enjoyed going through his mail and balancing his checkbook.

By early October, Jim asked me to stop allowing visitors outside of immediate family. However, when our young landscaper stopped by to do a long-agreed-upon small job, Jim asked to see him. Joe had designed our front yard and Jim was fascinated with his eye for design. He had watched Joe work from the front porch and Joe would spend his work breaks chatting with (and probably getting unsolicited advice from) Jim. When Joe stopped by to clean our gutters as a favor, Jim asked me to bring him into his room. Jim told Joe he knew I would have more work for him and that he appreciated how he had beautified our front yard. It meant a lot to Jim to have another task on his list of worries handled, namely cleaning the gutters, and to be able to see Joe one more time.

It was a matter of a few days before Jim had to stay in his bed full-time. Due to Jim's loss of strength, we had a very difficult transfer to the bathroom and he refused to use a bedside commode. Ultimately, I had to quite firmly tell him I could not risk transferring him any longer. One of us would be hurt, I explained, and it would make things much more difficult for both of us.

"How will I go to the bathroom?" he asked, alarmed. When I explained he would have to use the incontinence undergarments, Jim was horrified. I had Jo speak with him about it to reinforce my position. The next couple times he needed to urinate, he begged me to take him to the bathroom. I spoke to him calmly and promised the caregiver and I would keep him clean. Not only that, I said, his bed was set up to accommodate this. He complained but eventually could no longer hold his urine. After a time or two, he could go in his sleep and did not seem to be aware when he was actually urinating. I don't know if there was any bowel blockage or if it was because he only ingested liquid for so long, but Jim never did have a bowel movement in bed.

Another fear Jim had to overcome was receiving a bed bath. We talked about whether he would prefer a male or female nurse, and I agreed to stay in the room with him. The female hospice aide was respectful, self-assured, and efficient. Jim gripped my hand tightly and looked away as she began, talking reassuringly and explaining what she was doing. When she offered Jim the washcloth to address his personal zone, I sensed that a barrier came down. By the end of the process, Jim was pleased how easily he had been refreshed, his bed had been changed, and fresh clothes had been put on. On the next visit from the aide, I offered to stay and Jim said it wouldn't be necessary. I left them closing the door but listening for a minute. The chatter was friendly and it was clear Jim had accepted the aide for her professionalism.

One afternoon I was dusting in his room and stealing glimpses of Jim's peaceful face as he slept. The music he had come to like played softly, a beautiful day outside the window. I just enjoyed being near him, even if he needed to sleep more than he needed me to chit-chat with him. I turned back to dusting and suddenly there was a noise from the bed that made me smile and turn around. For several years we had this affectionate signal where Jim would make this flirty, tongue-clicking noise and we would both laugh. When I swirled around in surprise to see Jim grinning at me, I burst out laughing for the first time in quite a while. In his gravelly, soft voice, he said, "I can still make you laugh." It was a sweet moment for both of us.

Now that Jim was in bed full-time, I needed help with his care. Though aid from hospice caregivers a couple times a week helped tremendously, I decided to hire a morning caregiver to lighten my load so I would have enough strength in reserve for evening. Mostly I was concerned about keeping Jim comfortable in bed without hurting my back, as he would slide or shift and need to be re-positioned. I hired a daytime caregiver from an agency to assist me with shifting Jim in bed, to spend time with him as needed, and to assist with his personal care between visits from the hospice caregiver. Jim liked the first caregiver and she seemed suited to the work. When she took another job closer to her home, we hired another person through the agency. The replacement, promoted as highly qualified, was not. Her experience was working in a skilled nursing facility. Her English was so limited she did not understand instructions. She worked frantically, which was unsettling to Jim. That she cleaned the bathroom sink with the toilet bowl brush was unsettling to me, so she was gone after the second day. Due to a hallucination, Jim also came to think she was doing something inappropriate (not true) but I was glad to have legitimate reasons to replace her and solve the problem of his unfounded claims at the same time. His hallucination was due to his decline, not the morphine.

The next caregiver, though more suited to the slower and quieter pace of hospice patients, was horrified when told Jim was not being fed solid foods. She seemed unconvinced that he would be sick and in more distress if he was fed. She eventually came to understand just how sick he was when she saw how he labored to cough or, occasionally, vomit.

One afternoon I found Jim struggling in bed, having removed all his clothes and seeming to be in an altered state of consciousness. When asked, he told me he was getting dressed for work. Rather than argue that he no longer worked, I decided to go with his current state of mind to reassure him. I gently explained to him that he was not scheduled to work that day and that he could stay in bed and rest. He calmed down after repeated reassurances. He ultimately decided he did not want to wear clothing any more, except the underwear. This is not an unusual choice for individuals who are dying. I would draw a sheet over him but advised his daughters that he might feel the need to be uncovered at some point.

Another evening, I checked on Jim before sitting down to eat dinner. I made sure the rail was up on the bed and that his favorite New Age music was playing softly before I closed the door so the dog would not try to jump on the bed. A few minutes later I heard a noise and Jim had climbed over the rail and fallen out of bed, resulting in his arm being caught up in the rail. I grabbed the telephone, opened the garage door so the EMTs and fire department team could find their way in, and returned to Jim's side. He thought he had to go to work again and tried to climb out. He was clearly in pain, so I freed his arm as quickly as possible and called hospice to send help. I sat on the floor with Jim, bracing his body against mine and covering him with a blanket. His bony body would have been more bruised if

I had left him lying on the floor but I knew better than to try to lift 160 pounds. The local rescue team came in just a few minutes and lifted Jim easily into bed, ending the upsetting episode.

Jim would continue to watch television and open his mail, but was no longer able to make sense of the words. He was finally convinced to let me take over balancing his checkbook. He wanted control but would cry and become depressed if he could not get the book balanced. I told him he was too tired to focus and that I would balance the checkbook and show it to him. I guess I would describe his response as reluctant relief. It was another loss of capacity, but he trusted me to do my best to carry on for him. Jim would also hand items from the mail over to me after he opened them and tell me what to do, though some of the instructions did not make sense. He would express annoyance if I did something he didn't like, such as opening a letter with my finger instead of the letter opener, for which I would apologize. After a taxing activity like opening the mail, he would sleep, music playing softly to hold his attention and distract from outside noise.

As Jim became weaker, his voice began to fade. It was becoming harder and harder for him to express himself audibly and he required assistance to cough up mucus stuck in his throat several times each day. It became obvious the nutrition drink, which was milk-based, contributed to this problem. He had been resisting it anyway, so it seemed more acceptable to supply only popsicles and eliminate the nutrition drinks that made his coughing fits worse.

One of his last verbal communications to me was a request for me to remember to send a substantial donation to North County Hospice for all their help. Though it was increasingly hard to converse with Jim, his daughters continued to spend time with him.

Roberta would bring pictures and massage his feet. When she gave him several frozen bars in a row and I commented, Jim put me in my place. "What's it going to do, kill me?" I was glad he still had a scrappy sense of humor, even if it was dark humor.

THE SANDS OF TIME RUN LOW

Renee often found it difficult to get her father's attention during visits. It seemed to her he was ignoring her to watch television or fall asleep, which he also did to me much of the time. I felt bad for her because she wanted nothing more than to have meaningful visits. She asked her father if he had questions or concerns about spiritual matters and if he wanted her to pray with him. Jim was open-minded but non-committal about religion so he welcomed her prayers.

Family visits had begun to take a bigger toll on his energy and I was seeing signs on Jim's body that he was changing physically in ways that signaled greater decline. At this point, Jim was struggling to enjoy visits even from his daughters, so I asked the family to stay away for the weekend. He needed time to be quiet and sleep undisturbed. Surely, it wasn't what they wanted to hear, but I explained we all needed to remember this was about their father and not what we thought would keep him here. During those few days, Jim took new steps toward his transition.

That weekend he awoke from a morning nap to tell me he had seen some deceased family members. I asked what that was like and he told me it scared him at first. His voice continued to fade as Jim struggled to get breath to talk and to recover from coughing spells to clear his airways. I would put my ear close to his mouth to hear what he was saying. After a quiet weekend, and about ten days before he passed, Jim asked for his brother. Dennis, who cared for his wife Karen, a stroke victim, came up right away to say goodbye. Jim also had a very good visit with Renee, who excitedly asked me for some nail polish to fulfill his request.

"Paula, I think Dad is channeling Grandma. Remember when I used to put red polish on her nails and she liked that? Dad asked me to put red polish on his nails," she said, excited to be communicating with him.

I provided several colors of nail polish, thinking Jim might not have realized there were options other than red. I then left the two of them to do whatever was making them happy. About twenty minutes later, I stopped in the room to see Jim admiring his hands. "Cool," he noted with a raspy whisper and a smile. He apparently thought better of going with red and had chosen a shade of green. I wondered if it reminded him of money or perhaps his green camo hunting gear. I have no idea what brought about his request, but clearly Renee and her father had a lovely time together that afternoon and Jim seemed very satisfied. The next day, seeing her father had made a new fashion statement, Roberta finished the job by giving him green toenails to match.

A few days later Jim began waking in the morning to ask if he was "dead yet." He sobbed deeply when I replied he was still with me. This happened several times and I cried for him, too. Clearly, he was emotionally ready to cross over. One of his last conscious acts was to ask the entire family to gather around his bed. Dennis again made the trip, though he thought he had already said goodbye, and we waited for Renee's husband who had gone to a job interview unaware of the request. Once Jay arrived, the family held hands in a circle in the small den room while the girls sat next to their father as his unburdening began. He apologized for sometimes being less than an ideal father. After that, his weak voice made it difficult to hear most of what he said, beyond asking us to be good to one another.

As we all know, sometimes unexpected problems occur at the very worst times. Just a couple days before Jim died, I detected a leak in one of the walls. Panicked because we had previously experienced damaging leaks from the fire suppression system, I made some calls to find out how to quietly resolve the leak. Workers had to bring ladders into the hallway, just inches from Jim's door, but managed to work without Jim's knowledge. When told the problem could not be completely repaired without sounding the system alarms, which would have been disruptive and jarring to Jim, I decided to have the leak contained and cross my fingers. The repair company indicated the faulty pipes were vulnerable to excessive pressure, but I just prayed we could hold off until Jim was gone. Fortunately, the service companies were compassionate and worked out temporary fixes that held until the most important matters were handled.

Jim would now move his lips, but little if anything came from his vocal cords. I finally explained to him that he had done a wonderful job of taking care of me and his family, setting us up for more secure futures. He had shown me all I needed to know and I appreciated how much he cared, but now it was time for him to rest. At one point, as though thinking of one last thing he needed to communicate, Jim's arms waved wildly until I figured out he wanted pen and paper to write a message. I brought them but he could only make strange scribbles on the paper. When there was something to say or do, it was Jim's habit to do so without delay. It was hard for him to let go of business. Again, I told him he had handled everything, including making sure I knew how much he loved me. Soon he was asleep, never to awaken again.

SIGNS DEATH IS NEAR

Within the final weeks of life, the muscles of the body rapidly weaken, importantly including the swallowing muscles. Limiting solid foods and then fluids is advised once swallowing is further impaired. If fluids containing milk, such as nutritional milk-based supplements, are ingested during this time, the mucus can thicken and become even more difficult to cough out when muscles are already weak, so eliminating milk products is advised. Repetitive, ineffective coughing can be heard in the final week, and the caretaker can reduce coughing by positioning the patient on their side, rather than their back, as well as gently helping to clean the oral cavity.

Another common physical change is louder breathing sounds; sometimes loud gurgling accompanies changes in breathing pattern, often with spaces in the breathing pattern. The body temperature can rapidly alternate from cool to warm, so you may feel sweating, then shortly thereafter, cool skin. The skin of the hands and feet may change color to blotchy red or purple. Urine will darken with reduced volume. Confusion may develop into varying degrees of restlessness, and sleeping becomes perpetual. All of these normal changes should be described by the hospice nurse and all are in the book many hospices distribute to their families called Gone from My Sight *by Barbara Karnes, RN.*

Death and Family Dysfunction

Hospice work has shown me how the impending death of a parent is a direct threat, a crisis, in an already hurting, conflicted family. As the dying person weakens to the point of being bedfast, with increased needs for physical care and comfort medications, some family members may now react with strong emotions related to widely divergent and often inappropriate ideas of how to interact with the dying person. Bad behavior may erupt. Years of stored-up emotions in families who have kept secrets, childhood hurts which have never been aired and healed, and old sibling rivalries suddenly rise up, exploding into what should be a peaceful space for the dying to process their transition.

For example, when the patient requires quiet solitude to process his/her past and work toward resolution and peace, a family member may insist on talking to and stimulating the patient to converse. When a patient begins having muscular discomfort with the long periods of bed rest, another relative may loudly protest the small amounts of liquid morphine given for pain relief and to ease breathing. Another family member who has not been part of the care team or who is unfamiliar with hospice may insist on trying to feed a patient who has lost interest in nutrition.

For an aged patient, the hospice team is required under Medicare regulations to meet the needs of the patient and family, so problems such as these will be assessed by the hospice social worker. Many psycho-social problems can be mitigated with the assistance of the hospice social worker, chaplain, and nurse. Sometimes having the medical director meet with a family member who is unrealistic about the goals of care can be offered to clear up misunderstandings. Hospice team family meetings are offered to assist troubled families through some of the rough passages of the dying process. Ideally, families will make strides healing old patterns before a loved one dies, thereby preventing ruptures and estrangements that would last for the remainder of their lives. Sadly, some families are so invested in dysfunction they will continue squabbling beyond the death of a loved one, perhaps interfering with asset distribution, litigating against siblings, or worse.

OUR FINAL GOODBYE

In the few days that first week of November 2013 during which he was in a full comatose state, Jim's daughters had shorter, quieter visits with their father, but more time was spent in the dining room talking among family members. We obtained supplies from the pharmacy to keep Jim's mouth moisturized. We chose our words carefully when we were in his room, as hearing is the last sense to leave the dying. I invited the hospice social worker to join us and be available as a resource to the family. This time was a mix of questions, emotions, smiles, tears, and sharing memories.

On the day that I felt would certainly be Jim's last, I said nothing to the others. After all, I could be wrong; it didn't seem necessary to alarm his family when emotions were high. I was quite sure Jim would approve of my approach to keep the focus on his desire for a quiet, gentle conclusion to his life. That night, even our little dog Lily-Lou knew something was changing. She had not been allowed even supervised visits on Jim's bed for several days but clearly did not want to leave his room when we entered together so I could check on Jim that night about 10:00 p.m. She sniffed and struggled to free herself of my arms to be beside Jim. I put her outside the door so I could make sure he was tucked in. I said my goodbyes and a prayer before gently closing the door. I carried Lily to my bed, closing that door, as well. I got up every two hours to check on Jim and give him his meds, as I had done for several nights. I don't know how or why, but I was able to get up and then promptly drop back to sleep each time. At 6:00 a.m., I knew he was gone before opening the door to his room. Lily's behavior told me she knew, too.

When I entered the room the morning of November 7 with Lily-Lou in my arms, Jim was no longer breathing and his body was cooling, but he looked peaceful. His presence was still palpable so I talked to him for a few minutes about how life and death were simultaneously taking us both to new places. After telling him I would always love him and wishing him happiness in his final home, hospice was my first telephone call.

VIGIL OR ABSENCE?

A recommendation when death seems imminent is for family to allow the dying person a small portion of each hour to be alone. For unknown reasons, some individuals will die only when loved ones are out of the room. One belief is that the dying person senses the energy of loved ones and may be reluctant to leave while they are present. If you remain in the room and there is a change in breathing, such as soft gasps or "fish out of water" breathing, that may signal that death is minutes away. The chest may collapse downward and not rise again. These natural signs do not occur with every person, yet it is important to be aware they are natural signs that respiration is about to cease. Once the breathing has ceased, the face may quickly turn pale and waxy, and the eyes will seem glassy.

Once death is known to those gathered, the family's grief unfolds and crying ensues for most. Hospice is the only call that needs to be made. There will be immediate support for the bereaved while an RN will prepare and cleanse the body, notify the mortuary, dispose of medications safely, and notify the attending physician.

MY FIRST DAY WITHOUT JIM

After calling hospice, I made two pre-planned calls to my dear friends Chris and Carol. They had agreed to come spend the first night with me. By the time they arrived later that morning, I had assisted a hospice nurse in washing Jim's body, which was then delivered to the funeral home. I also managed to get quick calls in to my other closest friends and family, who were relieved that I would not be alone. A bit later that day, I had an appointment at the funeral home and Carol stayed behind while Chris and I went to make the arrangements.

Once the business was completed, the funeral director took a few minutes to chat and was thoughtful enough to tell me how his conversations with my husband had informed him of my husband's love for me. It didn't surprise me that Jim would say such things to someone outside our immediate circle, but it is something I never tired of hearing. The next moment, I suddenly remembered the green nail polish and thought I should say something. It is a small town, though I knew the funeral director would be discreet.

"You know, it was still sort of dark when I came in this morning and I thought to myself that I'd never seen that happen to anyone's fingernails before," he said. We had a good laugh and I explained that Jim's toenails were also green. Since that time, I have shared and laughed over the conversation at the funeral home many times. I still believe Jim's unique mani-pedi request so close to his end of life was a sweet form of communication with his girls, a memory to be cherished, even if others might think it peculiar coming from such a manly guy.

After a nap that first day, I shared a nice dinner cooked by my friends and we sat talking for hours. At bedtime, I prepared their sleep spaces and took Lily with me to Jim's den. The sheets had been removed so I put fresh ones on the "electric bed." Lily and I slept snuggled there that night, both of us feeling close to Jim in the place where we last saw him in our home.

MY FIRST WEEK ALONE

I slept well that first night and was happy to have cheerful gal pals in the house the next morning. We had such a good day that Carol and Chris agreed to stay another night. They are always easy to be with and never made me feel pitied. The talk was about memories, good times, lessons, and our love for one another. They helped me make plans for the next several days and I prepared a list of what I needed to do. There would be many telephone calls to make, most of a personal nature, and some of a business nature.

After calling a number of friends and family members over the course of several days, I finally could no longer muster the motivation to complete the list. It seemed to get harder with each call rather than easier. I finally telephoned my older brother, Stuart, and asked him to call our relatives that I had not contacted. Being on the other side of the country, he seemed to be happy to know of a way to help me out and I was grateful he took on a task that was wearing on me.

During this time, I received calls from hospice to check on me and cards began to come in from doctors and medical personnel who had been so instrumental in helping Jim through his cancer journey and final months. Flower arrangements brightened the house and the notes of condolence reminded me how many friends Jim had and had made even as he was dying. My frame of mind was one of gratitude to all who had helped us, as well as for the two years Jim and I had been given to say goodbye. After his passing, Jim's brother, Dennis, told me something Jim had shared with him years before he became ill. The conversation may have taken place during one of their many hunting and fishing trips and the subject was how they wanted to die. Jim had told Dennis he hoped he would have time to put his affairs in order once told he would die. I had never heard Jim say that, but it sure worked out that way for him. Though he had difficulties, had he died suddenly, I believe he would not have achieved the resolution he desired.

FIRST MONTHS: A TIME TO GRIEVE

At the start of Jim's journey, I cried so much that I had already done a lot of grieving work. Had Jim's death been sudden and unexpected I'm sure I would have cried more after his passing. When those moments did hit, they came on suddenly and without warning. I recall occasionally breaking down while watching television, Lily-Lou coming to my side from her window chair to comfort me. She seemed particularly upset if my sobbing came from deep within, resulting in that involuntary keening that is so painfully cleansing. She would gingerly approach to sit next to me and put one paw on my leg, then lick my arm or rest her chin on my leg.

At other times, a song on the car radio would unexpectedly trigger a flood of tears. Even when I sang along to a favorite song, I could instantly burst into tears if remembering the last time I sang it was with Jim. For the safety of others on the road, I would try to stifle these outbursts quickly, but would find the feelings returning to me throughout the day.

Exhausted from nearly two years of caregiving and the weather having turned cold, I was not in a hurry to bury Jim. It was some time before I would make that decision, but I decided to accept his ashes and keep some in a small urn, along with some locks of his hair I had saved from a haircut. The small urn was kept at home and the other cremains were stored until burial was imminent. I just did not know when that would be and asked the family to be patient with me while I figured out what seemed to be the right time.

When my soul sister, Janine, came to visit in January 2014, we celebrated both her and Jim's birthdays and I was in a good place to laugh and sob with her. But mostly we laughed and drank expensive wine she purchased. It was a very healing time to have a trusted loved one to unburden myself on about two months after Jim passed and I enjoyed her regaling me with the story of her "date" with Jim when I worked late that time a year before.

It was also during this time that Jo and I embarked on a personal friendship, as Jim had suggested. I first called to ask if she would go to dinner with me, joking that I thought she would understand if I became emotional. Around Jo I felt relaxed and had a chance to learn things about her that I was not able to learn when her relationship was strictly professional. The first summer we even took a little car trip together and continued making social plans thereafter. Jo was instantly liked by anyone I introduced her to, so it was fun to include her in my mix of friends.

For the most part, I was happy and dealing with life pretty well, even making new friends. While pipe leak repairs were completed immediately following Jim's death, I decided to invest in updating the house. Not only did that process busy me with interesting things to do, I became friends with my general contractor, Sammy, and his lovely family. Once finished, I incorporated mementos of my life with Jim to remind me of my many blessings.

Lily-Lou seemed to know just what to do in those early days, for she also missed Jim. Once or twice in the early months, I noticed her watching something in the room intently. Her head would then slowly turn as she kept watch of something moving. I asked her if she was seeing "Daddy" and her tail would thump a couple times, but she would remain still. I would greet him and invite him to stay as long as he wished.

COMFORTING THE BEREAVED

Grief is the universal, natural response of shock and sadness to the loss of an essential attachment such as a loved one. Bereavement is the process of grieving for the lost love, and is also experienced when a pet, job, or home is lost. The grieving process is as individual as each person and has no known timetable of duration. Hospices provide grief counseling and remain in contact with families to offer it every few months after the death of a patient. Most hospices provide one-one-one counseling for a few weeks near the beginning of bereavement. If needed, group counseling may be offered after the individual sessions end.

Grief at first can feel overwhelming, disorienting, beyond any pain one has yet survived. One may feel the ground of one's life has been swept away, without any sense of boundary or security. Swirling physical and emotional sensations such as stomach pains, absence of appetite, breathing problems, insomnia, extreme fatigue, numbness, fearfulness, hostility, intense loneliness, confusion, and more may erupt.

Bereavement, usually most intense at first, loses strength over time, as illustrated by an arc. As time moves on the bereaved may cry less often, but also unexpectedly. Sudden bursts of grief may occur at unforeseen moments such as in the post office where you last mailed that letter to the deceased loved one or when turning the corner near the house where they lived. If the bereaved remain present with their feelings, actually feeling them when they bubble up, they are likely to move through the bereavement process more smoothly, gradually finding their bearings. Then, only occasionally, such as when a major holiday approaches, similar profound emotions can rise up and briefly feel overwhelming again.

The bereavement process lasts as long as it takes. Eventually, this loss finds a new place in your life as you slowly adjust to the loss and resume living in a different way from the way you lived before the loss. You may discover you have new strength, feelings of independence, or urges to follow a new passion. You may develop warm connections to new people.

For those who find themselves in a position to offer comfort and support to the bereaved, consider these proven ways to better interact with a grief-stricken friend:

Share a fond recollection you have of the deceased.

Ask about the deceased's final days and whether that time is still very hard for the bereaved to deal with.

Offer to take a meal to them or invite them to music or a movie. Specifically name something you can do for them.

Avoid pat phrases like "time will heal" or "it's God's will" or offering your religious beliefs unless you know they are compatible with the bereaved one's beliefs.

Listen open-heartedly to their pain and acknowledge it without pity.

Offer warm affection, if welcomed.

Finally, if you find the bereaved person has been doing things that are harmful, or if they are constantly, month after month, preoccupied with the memory of their lost loved one, encourage them to seek help from a professional. (If the loss was unexpected and sudden, the bereaved are more likely to require professional help.) Therapists say that grief becomes complicated when people recycle their feelings with no resolution or they do things harmful to themselves and are preoccupied with grief for extensive periods of time. A mental health or hospice bereavement professional will assist in guiding them in healthier directions.

MY FIRST SOLO CHALLENGES

The funeral at Sacramento Valley National Cemetery in Dixon, CA on the first anniversary of Jim's passing was dignified and beautiful. He had been clear that his "Slice of Life" celebration was for non-family members and that his funeral would be for family only, so I knew it would make Jim proud to have just his family gathered to quietly mark his passing. My older brother Stuart and sister-in-law Fran were able to make the trip. Stu helped officiate the ceremony and lead prayers. Jim's brother, Dennis, spoke to the family in his reliably straightforward and humorous manner. I was touched when Jay's son and Renee's step-son, Nick, placed a memento from a charity run that he had dedicated to Jim in the container, along with the rose that represented the girls and me from the family wreath. Looking at our family gathered in the open-air structure I could not help but think Jim would have been happy, especially with his three grandchildren. Derek was forging his own way in the world, experiencing life and learning about becoming a responsible adult. Much younger, Jack was a bright, athletic, and good-natured teen. Preteen Ella was smart, effusive, and a fearless flyer on her cheer team.

After "Taps" was played and the ceremony ended, we were led to the newer section of gravesites where Jim was to be laid to rest. I was grateful for my brother to be present, especially as my other brother Stephen was unable to attend, and also because I had arranged to be buried alongside Jim when my own time comes. I wanted Stuart to see that place, in case he is unable to do so in the future. Before we left, I lowered Jim's ashes into his designated gravesite. As soon as the cemetery workers covered his remains, I finally felt a sense of completion in caring for Jim. His grave is located very close to where his parents had been buried in 2012. We said our goodbyes to Jim and lingered a few minutes at the graves of the girls' grandparents before heading home. That is a tradition we continue each time any of us visits the cemetery in our travels to Reno or the Sierra.

One of the most difficult things for me to do over the course of 2014 was to keep up with a small job I had been doing for a local newspaper. For some reason, my love of writing had disappeared. I struggled to come up with ideas for my column and the news stories required many more hours than they should have for me to craft them into something readable. Having enjoyed a thriving writing career for many years, I had slowly given up most of my newspaper, magazine, and business clients to focus on family, starting with Freda's care. I'd made my mind up to stick with writing for the local paper a while back but decided to abandon that last, now joyless vestige of my writing business at the end of 2014.

In November 2014, I followed my doctor's advice to go in for my regular colonoscopy. I followed that with my regular mammogram just to get all that out of the way and with intent to start the next year off with a clean slate. All was fine in the gut, but the mammogram came back showing an irregularity in my right breast for the first time in my life. At sixty-two, I was sure it was just a simple blip and that I would be able to nip the problem in the bud. A second screening led to a lumpectomy, which had to be repeated. Diagnosed with ductal carcinoma in situ and the doctor unable to get clear margins, I quickly made the decision to have a bi-lateral mastectomy. After all, it was considered by the doctors highly likely the left breast would become involved at some point. I did not want to experience the awkwardness of one missing breast and I really just wanted the entire cancer experience behind me so I could get on with life. Besides, one of my greatest fears was cancer treatment—radiation or chemotherapy.

My breast surgeon at UVMC recommended I go to Stanford as I indicated a desire for reconstruction and she felt they were best equipped to provide for my needs. I had wonderful care at Stanford, but my recovery was not without complications and discomforts. I never developed a "Why me?" sense of self-pity, but I recall thinking it would have been nice to have had a partner for comfort. Then I remembered Jim was not especially fond of caregiving and would have probably been pretty unhappy, so it was just as well. The one time I had been sick enough to need his help at home, I had the audacity to fall ill when he was to leave for a hunting trip. I never heard the end of that one.

God love my friends; Chris spent many days with me at the hospital and several friends, including Dee, Antonella, and Debbie, accompanied me on the two-plus-hour drive for doctor appointments. Family and other friends were in constant communication and sent prayers when they could not be present. During the next eighteen months, I took my time between surgeries trying to return to strength after each one. I insisted my soul sister, Janine, wait to visit from Chicago area until I was sufficiently recovered to have a really good time with her. By late Spring 2016 my Stanford treatment ended and the beginning of a slow recovery of my capacity began.

MOVING ON WITH HELP FROM JIM

Since my husband passed away in November 2013, there have been numerous instances when I felt Jim's presence or when he clearly communicated with me. This is something I wanted to ask him to do before he passed, but was always afraid he would consider the request to be self-serving or macabre. Many readers won't like or believe what I am about to describe in terms of psychic experiences, but they have provided comfort to me, so I share them.

The first overt instance of contact occurred Valentine's Day 2014; Jim had been gone just over three months. I slept in that morning and heard the phone ring in the kitchen and the message playing out loud as it was being recorded. It was ten o'clock and I could not recognize the voice or understand the message coming through on the kitchen base station, but suddenly I did recognize the tune to "Let Me Call You Sweetheart."

Hm. That's ironic, I thought, smiling. Jim had hired a barbershop quartet to come to the house to sing to me Valentine's Day 1999 when he proposed. The song I remembered from that surprise proposal was the one now on the voicemail recording. Curious, I finally roused myself from bed a few minutes later and went into the kitchen to play the message. The message was a "thank you" from a non-profit

Native American charity that Jim had supported with regular small donations throughout the years we were together. "Curtis," who made the call on behalf of the charity (his voice probably pre-recorded), did not ask for a donation, but said he wanted the children, "the little sweethearts" he called them, to thank us for Jim's support. Then a very crackly recording of the children's voices in song was played. It sounded like something from an episode of *The Twilight Zone*, as though it was being sent from outer space. How interesting. And so nice that it came at ten because Jim never liked to wake me up if I was sleeping, even if my alarm had not gone off and I had an appointment.

I played the recording for several friends and for Jim's daughter, Renee, who said it gave her chills. Some wondered if Jim had set the message up, which of course he did not—consciously. I believe he took some actions in his life that made this come about, and that it was more than a coincidence. Like people who see butterflies after a loved one passes and take that as a message, I believe I was being reminded of that special marriage proposal. Our marriage was something of which both of us were proud. That was but one incident that seemed a direct communication from my beloved husband since his passing.

Most of 2014 and 2015 were devoted to taking time for myself and not establishing too much routine. I took a few trips to visit friends and family, especially my mother's sister, Aunt Edna, but mostly stayed close to home. I amused myself by updating and redecorating my home and yard. I stayed in touch with Jim's daughters to check in and see how they were doing. I would notify them when there was a hospice or Veteran's remembrance in the event they wanted to join me in contemplating our loss and gratitude. I purchased a brick imprinted with information about Jim's military service on a new memorial in my community so the family would have a nearby place to remember Jim. By late 2015, I was beginning to feel bothered that I had not started on the book Jim wanted me to write about our hospice experiences.

In January 2016, I mentioned the book to Jo and my need to start writing. She commented she probably had some stories and professional advice to write about that would be helpful to hospice families. That's when I jumped on the opportunity to ask if she would join me. It seemed to me the book would have more impact with her input so I was delighted when she agreed. It took us a couple months to work out the direction and focus of what we needed to say, but working together was stimulating. We both had an imperative to share this information in the hopes of helping others.

Interesting to me as I look back, it seemed Jim became more active in communicating with me at this time. I was visiting with my friend Chris at my dining table on March 31, 2016. We discussed ideas for art to possibly accompany this book or a website supporting it. In a corner of the dining area is an antique cabinet that Chris and her fine furniture maker husband had updated for my recently redecorated home. The flag from Jim's military funeral ceremony, along with his ashes and a few mementos, is displayed through the glass front of the cabinet, which has a light in the top that I sometimes turn on for additional ambient light in the room. The cabinet light had not been turned on for weeks, but Chris suddenly noticed the light was on. I went over to turn it off and we turned back to our conversation, noticing a few minutes later the light was on again. I tried one more time to turn it off and it came back on when we weren't looking again. At this point, we invited Jim to stay and join the meeting. I left the light on until later that afternoon and it stayed off when I turned it off that time. The next day, April 1 or April Fool's Day, the light came on as I ate my breakfast. I had to laugh because Jim's mother had passed in the early hours of April 1, 2009. Freda was a jokester, so I always thought she would be amused by that date for her death anniversary, and now it seemed she and Jim were playing with me to remind me of her passing and that they had reunited. To be safe, because the cabinet lights would become hot, I unplugged the cabinet light and now only plug it in when I want the light to be on. I must admit to being sufficiently intrigued by this phenomenon that I would have been really freaked out if the light came on again after the cabinet was unplugged. It felt like another *Twilight Zone* moment.

My hairstylist, Holly, led me to another conduit of communication with Jim, much to our mutual surprise. One Friday that April as I sat in her chair, she told me of a psychic she had met who intrigued her with accurate information. Holly's husband had passed nearly a decade before Jim and she was more of a seeker of psychic support than I.

My only previous experience with a psychic had been a visit given to me as a gift when I turned forty. It happened to be a reading that accurately predicted when I would meet Jim. "I don't know if this will be the last person you love," the psychic had said, "but this will be the *big* one." I was not seeking a relationship at the time and didn't give that part of her reading another thought until Jim and I had been dating for almost three months and were already committed to one another. I re-examined several things that psychic told me and decided there must be people with true abilities of this nature.

Holly would be visiting the psychic she met a few weeks earlier on the coming Monday. She told me some of the things the psychic referenced that intrigued her but also mentioned there was a reference to Valentine's Day. Since Holly and her late husband were not big on Valentine's Day, she discarded that and assumed it was another departed individual. She was mostly interested in her departed family members and taking her daughter Melissa along. I asked her to call me afterward and let me know how her reading went.

Monday afternoon, a somewhat excited and breathless Holly called. After reminding me why she was calling, she explained her excitement. "I have a message for you from Jim," she exclaimed.

"Remember when I told you the first time I met this psychic she kept saying something about Valentine's Day? Well, it was Jim."

Holly explained what was said that led to this conclusion. The psychic told her this person was coming through for someone she had spoken to in her salon the previous week. Holly then remembered that Jim and I became engaged on Valentine's Day. She had forgotten about the mysterious telephone recording on the Valentine's Day after Jim died. Holly said Jim is happy and that he wants me to "live my life," adding she had a recording I could listen to for the details. Within a week or so, I drove to Holly's salon and listened to the psychic's CD in my car. Near the end of the portion dominated by my husband, the psychic asked Holly to "tell me about the little black dog."

"Oh, they had a little black poodle, but BD died," Holly responded.

"I know," said the psychic. "I see them together."

That was all it took for me to be overcome with joy and relief that made me cry. I was still unable to speak when I walked the CD back to Holly and then left for home. Jim and BD together was a picture in my mind since Jim left and the psychic's remarks were very much in tune with my personal beliefs about death. So much comfort!

As of this time, I can only recall one dream about Jim. In it, he lay next to me in bed and held up a note for me to read. My dream-self marveled at how good he looked and how at peace he seemed to be. It did not occur to me to read the note. Instead, I took the fact that he could print legibly as a sign that he was healed since his last earthly attempt to write was not successful. What might the note have said? I love you? Quit spending money? Take good care of Lily-Lou? I hope I have that dream again.

In 2016 I was anxious to make some changes in my life and make more of a contribution to my community. I decided to run for city council. Even in a small town, it was a large undertaking. I had been an active council watcher for years in my role with the newspaper and had become hooked on things others found boring. Also, by September, Jo and I were about halfway through writing the book. Between the two of us, we were seeking affirmation on various aspects of our lives. We decided to seek out a psychic as Jo had never had a reading and I was curious if Jim or another family member would come through. I also thought I might get some insight into how my campaign was going. We selected a psychic medium other than the one Holly went to because I am a healthy skeptic and did not want to be misled by expectations.

This psychic lived in a manse surrounded by a vineyard. On the way from the car to the front door I advised Jo not to tell her anything but to let the psychic tell us what she was thinking. There is no way this psychic could have found any information about us in advance. Jim and I had different last names and we had placed nothing online about the book as of this time. What I did share with the medium is that Jo and I were working on a "project" together. She immediately knew it was a book and Jim promptly came through to tell her he was happy about our work. She added that, in addition to the subject of the book, Jim was most happy Jo and I had become friends and were working together. There you have it, the man who asked me to become friends with Jo while he was alive now affirmed his joy from the other side at his wish being fulfilled.

Jim remains in my life every day. Only on a few occasions have I experienced brief bouts of loneliness because aloneness has never been a problem for me. I see his image and some of his favorite things in my home, like the head of the beautiful deer that hangs in the hallway. I sometimes talk about him to the dog. She likes that and wags when I mention "Daddy." I look forward to him communicating with me again but am satisfied that if he doesn't do so, I already know we are both fine. I have so many memories of our years together, the last two years being especially abundant with lessons and love.

Because of Jim I am secure; I have beloved old friends and interesting new friends. My passion for living a life of meaning burns stronger because I can help Jim communicate with others about his appreciation for his time on this earth and his respect for the all-important end phase of life. Both of us are endlessly appreciative of the help provided by hospice to achieve these realizations.

"The dead are often just as living to us as the living are, only we cannot get them to believe it. They can come to us, but till we die we cannot go to them."
– Samuel Butler, British poet, c. 1888

CHAPTER SUMMARY

- Hospice patients may object to some of the accommodations required to keep them safe and comfortable, such as bedside commodes, etc. It is vital to be firm with them to protect the well-being of both patient and caregiver.

- Even as a patient lapses into deep sleep or unconsciousness, it is important for visitors to support a calm, relaxing space and to not talk about the patient within their hearing range. There is plenty of evidence we should speak directly to the unconscious patient while in the room, but only speak of them in another part of the home or facility.

- Hallucinations and confusion are typical for a dying patient as chemical changes take place within the body and brain. Some may mistake this natural phenomenon for a response to medications or morphine. If agitated, hospice can adjust prescriptions to calm the patient. If hallucinations are benign, listen to what the patient says rather than denying what they say.

- Loss of appetite is a natural part of dying. The patient is likely to take only liquids until such time as they slip deeper into unconsciousness. Hospice provides medications to keep the dying person comfortable. The pharmacy carries remedies to keep the dying person comfortable and their mouth moisturized when they can no longer sip liquids.

- At some point, as sleep increases, the hospice patient may see or "visit" loved ones "on the other side." It may be an uplifting or unnerving experience. If they are still able to speak, listen to what they say and offer calm reassurance appropriate to their beliefs.
- Many dying individuals choose to shed clothing in late stages. They may also pick at covers or make unusual requests. If requests are harmless, such as my husband's request of his daughter to apply nail polish, just comply without judgement. I did not take this as a sign my husband was gay or harboring secret desires, but instead that he wanted very much to relate to his daughters.
- Many individuals and families believe the dying should be monitored until they expire. Depending on the dying patient's nature, it can also be appropriate to leave them alone at the very end, after saying what needs to be said. As with Jim, the removal of loving energy from the room can make it easier for some patients to "let go" when they are ready.

Resources

BEREAVEMENT

Association for Death Education and Counseling
www.adec.org
Contains resources for coping with various losses

www.complicatedgrief.columbia.edu
Website offers resources to help treat unrelenting grief reactions

www.journeyofhearts.org
Website of support resources for those grieving losses

www.nhpco.org
Website has link for grief support videos and other resources

www.dougy.org
Website for grieving children and families with
podcasts and tip sheets for different ages

GRIEF SUPPORT

www.whatsyourgrief.com

www.grieving.com

www.thegrieftoolbox.com

www.losingyourparents.com

www.recoverfromgrief.com

www.thecompassionateFriends.com

www.navigatinggrief.com

www.adec.org/adec/Main/Resources/Coping_With_Loss/
ADEC_Main/Find-Help/CopingWithLossNew/Coping_With_Loss.
aspx?hkey=4205f831-6518-48e7-99d3-491ad28dee89

HOSPICE SUPPORT

The National Hospice and Palliative Care Organization
www.nhpco.org

The Hospice Foundation of America
www.hospicefoundation.org

HospiceNet
www.hospicenet.org

National Association Homecare and Hospice
www.nahc.org

National Hospice Foundation
www.nationalhospicefoundation.org

SPIRITUALITY AND RELIGION AT END OF LIFE

www.Spiritualityhealth.com/articles/what-dying-taught-me-about-living

www.huffingtonpost.com/kenneth-j-doka/spiritual-needs-of-the-dy_b_831123.html

Dedication

This book is dedicated to James Edward Ronlund, 1943-2013.
Son, brother, outdoorsman, veteran, husband, father,
friend, hospice supporter, and inspiration.

In support of hospice, 10% of the proceeds from the sale of this publication is given to hospice organizations.

You can help a hospice organization in your area with a donation to provide services for members of your community and their families.

The lyrics of this moving song written by Karen Brown, a Northern California songwriter and singer, touched me when I first heard it performed by Karen and Bootleg Honey, a wonderful group of talented women from my area of California. Karen was moved to write the song after watching strangers observe a celebration of life in a San Francisco public park, presumably a favorite place for the deceased.

GATHERING

Drink in the sun and feel the waves
Here is where we come to make your grave
Toss a rose into the wind
Tide will bring it out and in

We are gathered here today
To see you off in our strange way
Hand in hand a silent prayer
Send a message if we dare

(chorus)
Petals float on
Peaks and foam
Ever searching, searching for a home
Petals red and petals pink
Carry thoughts beyond the brink

Seems unfair to love it so
Golden bridge and the fortress old
Here is where we stood before
Together we beheld, beheld this very shore

First a visit, then to stay
Roots went deep beneath, deep beneath the bay
Rising up around you now
Those you loved like blooming flowers

(chorus)
Petals float on
Peaks and foam
Ever searching but they're never, never home
Petals pink and petals red
Join the living with the dead

Drink the sun, feel the waves
In our city by the bay

To hear the song Gathering, connect through Karen's website:
http://www.karenjoybrown.com/little_words_album/s/gathering

I was drawn to the music performed by Bootleg Honey because
their themes of joy, warmth, reflection, grouchiness, attraction,
and silliness are elements of life we need to allow into our days
as we move forward from loss so that hope is fully restored. Their
music will surely bring a smile to your face. Learn more about
Bootleg Honey and their music at:
https://www.facebook.com/bootleghoneymusic

– Paula

About the Authors

For more than twenty-five years Paula Wrenn worked as a freelance writer for newspapers and magazines. Older adults, caregiving, aging well, and hospice are among the many topics she covered based on earlier experiences as an elder-care business owner and a long-standing volunteer for local organizations serving seniors and individual senior adults. She currently is a board member serving her local health care center.

Paula has assisted several members of her family through the transition from life to peaceful death. She believes those who go before us provide valuable insights and guidance about living and dying.

"Caregiving for a loved one is challenging and stressful at times, but the rewards are immeasurable. *Dying Well with Hospice* is about validating the importance of end of life and helping families discover the spiritual and emotional benefits that can be attained by supporting a loved one in this most important journey, their transition to the next realm."

* * *

As a child, Jo Gustely was fascinated by taboo subjects including séances, death, and true ghost stories. Along the way, she considered careers as a mortician and forensic pathologist. As a young adult, she changed careers from ESL teacher to nursing. After obtaining her BA from UC Berkeley she earned her BSN from Emory University. Since 1985, she has been a post-surgical nurse, a home care nurse, a corporate occupational nurse, and a public health nurse.

Jo became a hospice nurse in Northern California in 2005. For her, hospice provides a perfect balance of challenges and benefits, including the opportunity to interact with different cultures and to work with inspiring team members from different disciplines outside the hospital setting. Competently and compassionately problem-solving to alleviate difficult symptoms for hospice clients is among the highly satisfying aspects of her work. She has witnessed many awe-inspiring moments of psycho-spiritual renewal for clients nearing the end of life and has been present for profound instances of family affection, love, and support of courageous hospice clients.

"Most people think it is a calling to be a hospice nurse, and I would say that I felt called to do this work because of the frequency with which I am privileged to share momentous experiences in people's lives."